LIBERALISM, NATIONALISM AND THE GERMAN INTELLECTUALS

LIBERALISM, NATIONALISM
AND THE
GERMAN INTELLECTUALS
(1822—1847)

An Analysis of the Academic and Scientific Conferences of the Period

BY

R. HINTON THOMAS

Lecturer in German
University of Birmingham

W. HEFFER & SONS LTD., CAMBRIDGE

1951

Printed in Great Britain at the Works of
W. HEFFER AND SONS LTD., CAMBRIDGE, ENGLAND

PREFACE

THE theme of this book is, I think, sufficiently indicated by the title and sub-title to require no preliminary comment, except perhaps to explain its chronological limits. The investigation proper begins in 1822 simply because in that year the first of the academic and scientific conferences took place; it ends in 1847, the year of the last to be held before the revolution of 1848. This is the first time that these conferences have been systematically analysed in the wider context of events and trends culminating in 1848, and to this extent at least my book can claim the virtue of novelty.

Two of the three series of conferences (Scientists and Doctors, Classical Philologists) continued after 1848, but in the changed circumstances they necessarily assumed a rather different function and character. This is one reason for restricting my enquiry to this early period of German liberalism. Another is that it is an important part of my argument that, in the sense suggested by the title of the Conclusion, this period is a key to later developments. In any case, the history of these and other conferences in the second half of the nineteenth century raises many new problems—no less important, but best treated separately. I shall not undertake this task, but it can be recommended as a field in which research could make a valuable contribution to German social history.

My primary sources have been the official proceedings of the different conferences. Included among my secondary sources have been a large number of memoirs, autobiographies, letters, etc. I have mentioned these only where they provided material directly incorporated in the text. In view of the variety of sources used, I have thought it unnecessary to provide a list of books to which reference has been made, especially as many are mentioned in footnotes.

I have been greatly aided in my study by grants on two separate occasions over the past four years from the Research Committee of the University of Birmingham. Without this help, and without a term's study-leave in 1948, I could not have completed my work. To the

authorities concerned I wish to express my deep gratitude.
It is a pleasure also to acknowledge my debt to the officers—
in particular Dr. W. M. Luther—of the Göttingen University
Library, who have helped me in every possible way with
their splendid resources.

To those who have helped individually I must record a
special debt to Professor Roy Pascal, who read my manuscript and made suggestions too numerous to mention,
and to Dr. S. F. Mason, of the University of Oxford, who
furnished me with valuable material, incorporated in
Chapter I, regarding the scientific congresses in Italy.

R. H. T.

BIRMINGHAM.

CONTENTS

                                               PAGE

PREFACE   V

INTRODUCTION. THE PROBLEM AND ITS SETTING ..   I

CHAPTER

  I   THE CONFERENCES OF SCIENTISTS AND DOCTORS   20

  II   THE CONFERENCES OF CLASSICAL PHILOLOGISTS, SECONDARY SCHOOLMASTERS AND ORIENTAL- ISTS   51

  III   THE CONFERENCES OF UNIVERSITY TEACHERS OF GERMAN LAW, GERMAN HISTORY AND GERMAN LANGUAGE ('GERMANISTEN')   ..   81

CONCLUSION. THE CRISIS OF GERMAN NATIONALISM   120

APPENDIX

  I   DATES AND PLACES OF CONFERENCES TILL 1848   139

  II   LIST OF MEMBERS OF THE 'GERMANISTEN' CONFERENCES   140

INDEX   147

INTRODUCTION

THE PROBLEM AND ITS SETTING

In a short essay published in 1922 Meinecke remarked
that 'the political views and activities of German scholars
form a peculiar historical pattern' and that 'their basis,
origin and development' deserve a careful assessment.[1]
Occasions when members of the intellectual middle class
met in organised gatherings would obviously provide
valuable evidence for a study of this aspect. If meetings
could be discovered which brought them together regularly
and systematically from many different parts of Germany
for the discussion of problems overlapping into questions
of politics and society—and if authentic records of the
discussions were available—they would furnish material
of the greatest importance. These conditions are fulfilled
by the congresses of German scholars, which took place
annually from 1822 to 1847; there were similar congresses
later, but this book is concerned only with those before 1848.
The example was set by the conferences of Scientists and
Doctors, who first met in 1822. It was followed (from
1838) by those of the Classical Philologists, Secondary
Schoolmasters and Orientalists, and in 1846 and 1847 by
the University Teachers of German Law, German History
and German Language; the last described themselves
collectively as 'Germanisten,' though the term has been
narrowed down in general practice to denote persons concerned with the study of German language and literature.
In each case the group of scholars concerned added the
word 'German' in their title (Conferences of German
Scientists and Doctors, etc.), but we shall omit this for the
sake of brevity. The main importance of all these conferences lies in the way in which they reflected the social
and political developments which reached their climax in
1848 and at the same time contributed to them.

[1] 'Drei Generationen deutscher Gelehrtenpolitik,' in *Historische Zeitschrift*,
125.

I

On the threshold of this early period of German liberalism stand the reforms instigated in Prussia by Freiherr vom Stein. When Prussia was defeated by Napoleon at Jena in 1806 and the effete Holy Roman Empire collapsed under the impact of the French revolutionary armies, Stein realised that it was no longer possible to rule exclusively through the nobility and bureaucracy, that Prussia's military eclipse was the consequence of social weakness. He therefore set out to widen the basis of the state by giving a more active share to the propertied middle class. In 1807 town-dwellers above a certain property-level were enfranchised and the towns granted a significant measure of self-government independent of the state administration. The army reforms led to the creation of a specifically bourgeois 'Landwehr,' a reserve army through which the middle class was able to play a part in the overthrow of Napoleon. As Meinecke observed, the 'Landwehr' was regarded, alike by its supporters and opponents, not merely as a military but also as a political institution, contributing towards the emancipation of the bourgeoisie.[1]

In 1815 the Congress of Vienna created the German Confederation, consisting, in addition to four Free Cities, of thirty-five sovereign states, subject only to the vague and ceremonial authority of the Confederation. This was a reduction as compared with the number of German states in the eighteenth century but it was in no sense a concession to German unity. Against this were ranged the advantages to foreign powers accruing from disunity and also the dynastic interests of the German princes. Similarly it was not the intention to make the Confederation a framework for the growth of democratic institutions. In Prussia hopes of constitutional democracy were aroused by several promises by Frederick William III, but these were disregarded as soon as the political situation was stabilised under the con-servative domination of Austria, whose influence during the nineteenth century was "due to the fact that she incorporated the spirit of resistance to change."[2] Austria was president

---

[1] Cf. his essay 'Landwehr und Landsturm,' in *Preussen und Deutschland*, Munich and Berlin, 1918, pp. 73-4.

[2] Roy Pascal, *The Growth of Modern Germany*, London, 1946, p. 4.

of the German Confederation, which was dominated by Metternich's idea that princes owed allegiance only to God. There were variations in government within the different states. In the socially and politically most backward—like Mecklenburg—the system was for all practical purposes feudal. It is true that in some states, in the south-west, elected diets existed, but their composition was relatively narrow and their powers were restricted.

The reactionary character of the Confederation and its divided political structure have an important bearing on the fact that from the time when the middle class contributed to the defeat of Napoleon, liberalism and nationalism in Germany went hand in hand in the bourgeois movement. The struggle for national unity was from the point of view of the bourgeoisie at the same time a struggle against the princes. The interests of the princes were intimately bound up with the small-state system; the preservation of their respective dynasties involved maintaining the separate sovereign states. Thus the campaign of the bourgeoisie for liberal rights and institutions involved quite naturally a struggle for unity. Moreover, the princes and nobility had identified themselves to a certain extent with foreign interests, and this aspect was thrown into relief after 1815 by the Concert of Europe, which was virtually an international conspiracy for the consolidation of the old order. The German Confederation was seen by liberal opinion in much the same light, and so a liberal clergyman of the time could describe it as "an instrument of permanent conspiracy by the separate governments against their subjects'[1] and against the unity of the nation. The possibility of such an alliance had been adumbrated by the aristocratic writer Eichendorff in his novel *Ahnung und Gegenwart* (completed 1811, published 1815), in which the Prince remarks that "our time is so violent that nothing is effective without power. The few courageous people from the whole world should therefore loyally stick together to form a veritable dam against evil.'[2]

[1] Willibald Beyschlag, *Aus meinem Leben*, Halle, 1896, p. 30.

[2] Bibliographisches Institut ed., II, p. 172.

In these circumstances the bourgeoisie could claim with a certain amount of justice that it represented 'German' interests, even before the growth of trade and manufacture gave it an added interest in the unification of Germany.

Napoleon had tried to force Britain to capitulate by imposing the Continental Blockade, the purpose of which was to cut her off from European markets and starve her into surrender. While the Continental Blockade was in force the German economy gained in some respects by being protected from British competition. Some factories, which before the Blockade suffered under the competition of British goods, enjoyed for a time greater prosperity. Though industries dependent on import or export were often hard hit, home industries tended to flourish. The Leipzig Fair of 1810 was one of the most successful so far held, the demand for the products of home industry exceeding the supply.[1] The textile industry of Saxony benefited considerably, replacing British yarn by its own manufacture.

The lifting of the Blockade after the defeat of Napoleon removed these advantages (though it added others). The German export market was exposed to the full force of British competition. This was felt all the more sharply since Great Britain was now in a position to unload on the German market the goods which had meanwhile accumulated. The fact also that Great Britain had not been ravaged by war was to her economic advantage. Moreover, in the meantime British industry had begun to benefit from the use of steam, the application of which she tried to monopolise during the years when war divided her from the Continent.[2] She poured her products into Germany at a time when Germany herself was in a state of depression. The figures for the period 1780–1822 for Great Britain's imports from and exports to Germany show that the value of exports greatly increased while the value of goods imported from Germany dropped from about one-half to

[1] Cf. H. G. Schenk, *The Aftermath of the Napoleonic Wars*, London, 1947, p. 84.

[2] Cf. J. H. C. Clapham, *The Economic Development of France and Germany, 1815–1914*, Cambridge, 1921, p. 4.

about one-tenth.[1] In 1832 a German liberal described the situation thus:

During the Continental Blockade and the continental wars the industry of Great Britain, which was in any case particularly favoured, increased continually. The consequence of the fact that her market had been only partially disturbed was an increased accumulation of manufactured goods. This exclusion of Great Britain also stimulated the productive effort of Germany. In the main, however, only the arts of war flourished. Moreover, these continuous wars themselves . . . withdrew the strength from all other branches of industry, which under the same system but in peaceful conditions would have blossomed rapidly. When the barriers fell . . . Germany was suddenly flooded with an immense mass of British goods, and her industry, which was only just beginning to recover, was again knocked to the ground.[2]

For a time Germany faced heavy odds in the struggle against British competition, but her powers of resistance gradually increased: 'The competition that we have to maintain with industrially more advanced nations compels us to follow as fast as possible.'[3] In 1835 Nebenius wrote:

The predominance of British industry was felt in its most oppressive form immediately after the restoration of the general peace. But the progress made in the art of production gradually became a common possession. On the Continent peace facilitated the accumulation of capital, and the great difference which had existed between the price of capital goods in Great Britain and the European states was more and more reduced. The competition of the North Americans, French and the Hansa states in sea trade, together with the progress in the availability of many products in various countries independent of Great Britain, weakened British predominance in regard to many raw materials. All these circumstances gradually made it easier for German industry to struggle against the effort of the British.[4]

Despite this advance, however, Germany's economic position by the middle of the century was considerably behind that of Great Britain or France. By 1830 only about one-third of Germany's population was urban and as late as 1840 large-scale factory enterprises of a modern kind were extremely rare, domestic industry—the most

---

[1] C. F. Nebenius, *Der deutsche Zollverein, sein System und seine Zukunft*, Karlsruhe, 1835, pp. 332–3.

[2] Wilhelm Schulz, *Deutschlands Einheit durch Nationalrepräsentation*, Stuttgart, 1832, pp. 69–70.

[3] *Ibid.*, p. 61.   [4] *Op. cit.*, pp. 337–8.

elementary form of capitalist production—predominating. The Rhineland was one of the areas where most progress was made. But, apart from the fact that it was specially favoured in communications and other respects, it was more closely linked to the economic orbit of Belgium, Holland and northern France than to Germany as a whole.

Yet in the first two or three decades after the Congress of Vienna significant changes took place in Germany's economic life, deeply influencing also the political situation. The establishment of the Customs Union in 1834 greatly stimulated the growth of internal trade and also marked the first significant stage towards the unification of Germany. The beginnings of a railway system in 1835 opened new possibilities of commercial development, and a few years later the King of Saxony remarked that they were 'one of the best means of consolidating a truly German outlook' and that they were desired by all the commercial towns in Germany 'out of a sense of pure patriotism.'[1]

These factors were markedly favourable to the advance of the bourgeoisie in Germany. As far as Germany is concerned, this was the period in which 'the philosophy of middle-class society' came to 'self-consciousness.'[2] In 1820 Hegel, for example, could assert in his *Philosophy of Right*: 'In the middle class are to be found consciousness of the state and the most advanced culture. For this reason it is the pillar of the state as far as uprightness and intelligence are concerned. A state in which there is no middle class is therefore not at a high stage of development. . . . It is one of the main interests of the state that this middle class is formed.' David Hansemann, a leading champion of the commercial interests of the bourgeoisie in the Rhineland, was at pains to show in 1830 that the majority in a nation cannot be defined merely by counting heads, that the 'true majority' consists of those who, because they have property, culture and knowledge, have the interests

[1] *Briefwechsel zwischen König Johann von Sachsen und den Königen Friedrich Wilhelm IV und Wilhelm I von Preussen.* Herausgegeben von Johann Georg, Herzog zu Sachsen, unter Mitwirkung von Hubert Ermisch, Leipzig, 1911, p. 192.

[2] Herbert Marcuse, *Reason and Revolution*, Oxford, 1945.

of the nation at heart, i.e. desire a strong and healthy government.[1] Dahlmann's generalisation in his *Politics* (1835) that 'almost everywhere in the world a widely distributed and increasingly homogeneous middle class forms the core of the population,' reflected the increasing self-confidence of the bourgeoisie in Germany as elsewhere. 'Every Government,' he declared, 'has to pay special heed to it, for in it is to be found at present the centre of gravity of the state and the whole body of the state follows its movement.' German liberals would for the most part have regarded it as self-evident that 'the prosperity of the middle classes is entirely bound up with that of the whole nation; and they are the only section of the community which is as yet deeply conscious of its relationship with the whole.'[2] 'It is necessary,' wrote J. G. Siemens in 1841, 'for the respect which the middle class desires . . . that it should not be held unfitted to administer the more important posts in the state.'[3]

This was a challenge to the aristocracy, which began to be portrayed in contemporary literature—as in Immermann's novel *The Epigoni* (1835)—as a dying class in a rising bourgeois age.[4] Hegelians—whose organ was Ruge's *Halle Year Books*—endeavoured to carry forward the revolutionary aspects of Hegel's thought, stressing 'that the core of this philosophy was not the system but the method, not rest but unrest, not that which is static but that which grows.'[5] The internal political development was much stimulated from abroad as a result of the July

[1] Quoted by Alexander Bergengrün, *David Hansemann*, Berlin, 1901, p. 109, from Hansemann's memorandum 'Über Preussens Lage und Politik am Ende des Jahres 1830' (sent to the King of Prussia dated December 31st, 1830, privately printed for delegates to the eighth Provincial Diet of the Rhineland in 1845).

[2] Roy Lewis and Angus Maude, *The British Middle Classes*, London, 1949, p. 282.

[3] Quoted from Siemens' *Die Elemente des Staatsverbandes*, Leipzig, 1841, by Karl Helfferich, *George von Siemens. Ein Lebensbild aus Deutschlands Grosser Zeit*, Berlin, 1921.

[4] For this aspect cf. E. Kohn-Bramstedt, *Aristocracy and the Middle Classes. Social Types in German Literature*, London, 1937.

[5] Franz Mehring, *Deutsche Geschichte vom Ausgange des Mittelalters*, Berlin, 1947, p. 165.

revolution in France in 1830. Unrest in some German states (Hesse, Hannover, etc.) was sufficient to lead the princes there to grant constitutions.

Influenced by these wider developments, German literature began to turn away from the fairy-world of Romanticism. Heine combined a sentimental affection for Romanticism with mockery of it. The school of writers known as Young Germany polemically introduced social and political themes to such an extent that the works of its leading members were banned by the German Confederation in 1835. With 1830 begins the modern political lyric which was one of the most characteristic expressions of the period. The writings of the dramatist Georg Büchner raised the issue of revolution and also the question of the proletariat.

Throughout the eighteen-forties the socialist idea, stimulated by the penetration (through the work of Lorenz Stein[1] and others) of French socialist thought, gained increasing influence through the writings of such men as Weitling and Hess. In 1847 the Communist League commissioned Marx and Engels to write its *Manifesto*. 'It is very bad,' wrote Wilhelm von Kügelgen, an artist of moderate liberal views, 'that a proletarian class is being formed which can acquire a *frightful significance*[2] and which can be drawn by restless minds into extreme measures. I sometimes feel as if the whole nation were standing by an abyss.'[3] But it was not only members of the middle class who sensed the dangers of social unrest. 'It is true,' said a conservative writer in 1835, rejoicing in Germany's relative economic backwardness, 'that industry and manufacture have (fortunately for the people) not made a sufficient advance to be linked up with great commercial and political catastrophes as in England and France.' But, he continued, 'forces have developed amongst us of which the eighteenth century had no inkling. . . . At the same time and as a result, however, the claims of those classes are increased which

---

[1] Cf. *Der Sozialismus und Kommunismus des heutigen Frankreichs*, 1842.

[2] Italicised by Kügelgen.

[3] *Lebenserinnerungen des Alten Mannes, 1840–1867*, Leipzig, 1925, p. 103.

participate in them and that in geometrical progression.'[1]

Some of the foremost intellectuals—such as Hegel, Immermann and Gutzkow—looked to the State as an effective means of reconciling the conflict between bourgeoisie and proletariat. In particular respects the attitude to the problem was influenced by conditions prevailing in different regions. The problem was acute in the Rhineland because of its comparatively advanced economic development. It was discussed, for example, by Karl Andree in some articles in 1844, entitled 'Industry and Society,' in the *Kölnische Zeitung*.[2] Drawing a moral from the social misery and unrest caused in England by rapid and unplanned industrialisation, he urged the need to decentralise production in order to avoid the concentration of workers in particular regions and so to ward off the conflict between capital and labour. Another approach was that of Karl Buhl who, writing from Berlin, advocated social welfare as a palliative.[3]

Turning to the political demands of the liberals on the home front, the most fundamental was for parliamentary democracy. There were various shades of opinion on this question, but they all had in common the idea that it was only through constitutional rights that people could be protected from the despotism of the princes and arbitrary interference by their bureaucracy. This demand was influenced both by the interests of the bourgeoisie as a class in the free development of trade and by fear of unrest among the masses. The result was the idea of a middle position supported by the authority of the state. This is well illustrated by the statement[4]: 'Our age strives for a strict legalism, and it is only for this reason that it seeks to achieve its aims through constitutions, the purpose of

[1] A. W. Rehberg, *Die Erwartungen der Deutschen von ihren Fürsten*, Jena, 1835, p. 25.

[2] For a summary of these articles cf. Karl Buchheim, *Die Stellung der Kölnischen Zeitung im vormärzlichen deutschen Liberalismus*, Leipzig, 1914, p. 286 seq.

[3] Cf. *Andeutungen über die Noth der arbeitenden Klassen und über die Aufgabe der Vereine zum Wohl derselben*, Berlin, 1845. For a short summary cf. G. V. Plekhanov, *In Defence of Materialism* (English edition, trans. Rothstein), London, 1947, p. 281 seq.

[4] Kügelgen, *op. cit.*, pp. 79–80.

which is to provide the guarantee of legalism. People want to get away from arbitrary rule. . . . Neither republics nor absolute monarchies are any use in Germany; what we need is firm and well-ordered power.'

These considerations throw light on the importance attached by the liberal intellectuals to public opinion. This was connected with the demand for parliamentary institutions, as Pfizer indicated when he wrote that 'the constitutional system demands publicity in the widest sense of the term.'[1] He spoke with authority, for he was among the leaders of the liberal opposition in the Württemberg Diet in the eighteen-thirties, author of the celebrated *Correspondence of Two Germans* (1831) and in March, 1848, Minister of Education in Württemberg. The summoning by Frederick William IV of the United Diet in Prussia in 1847 can serve as an illustration. As Eyck puts it, this 'was not the promised national representation. . . . But with all its drawbacks it was an immense step forward to constitutionalism for one reason: the King allowed the verbatim reports of the debates of the Diet to be published by the newspers, which had hitherto been forbidden by the censor to deal in any way with German or Prussian political affairs. Through the publication of these debates, the newspaper readers in Berlin or Magdeburg, Königsberg or Cologne, were for the first time able to read something about their own affairs. For a country without a free press it was an immense advance.'[2] A contemporary liberal said that 'the whole political life of free peoples is conducted in public in the same way as one inhales air.'[3]

This insistence on the value of public opinion and public discussion had both a negative and a positive aspect.

It was regarded as a safety-valve for the orderly release of energy and passion that might otherwise serve to exacerbate internal strife. Thus one observer wrote, reflecting widespread anxiety about the menace of a revolutionary proletariat: 'It is believed here also that, if the Estates can

[1] From his article 'Konstitution,' in the Welcker-Rotteck *Staatslexikon*, 3rd ed., III, p. 76 seq.

[2] Erich Eyck, *Bismarck and the German Empire*, London, 1950, p. 18.

[3] From the article 'Öffentlichkeit,' in *Staatslexikon*, X, p. 743.

maintain themselves as the organ of public opinion, Germany can escape the calamities by which she is now threatened.'[1] The same idea was formulated by Welcker when he said that institutions for the expression of public opinion were means 'by which violent explosions and evil *coups d'états*, such as revolutions, are prevented or recognised in their origins and disarmed.'[2] He added: 'In the nation . . . patriotic ideas and interests are bound finally to gain the upper hand. Therefore, if all the ways are open for the creation of this public opinion . . . it will maintain the organism of the state in controlled activity. If these means are impeded, first of all blockages, then sudden efforts, explosions, revolutions or death will be inevitable.'[3]

Positively, public opinion and public discussion were regarded as a way of securing the realisation of the liberal programme, sweeping away the restrictions of an effete social order and forcing through the changes which history had made necessary. 'Publicity,' said the liberal jurist Heinrich Simon in 1842, 'is the only protection against everything that is rotten in the state of Denmark.'[4] This aspect was pointed out by Engels when he asked: 'When interests so varied, so conflicting, so strangely crossing each other are brought into violent collision; when these contending interests in every district, every province, are mixed in different proportions; when, above all, there is no great centre in the country, no London, no Paris, the decisions of which, by their weight, may supersede the necessity of fighting out the same quarrel over and over again in every single locality; what else is to be expected but that the contest will dissolve itself into a mass of unconnected struggles, in which an enormous quantity of blood, energy and capital is spent, but which for all that remain without any decisive results?'[5] In 1843 Karl Rosenkranz, an East Prussian liberal, argued that political parties were necessary

[1] Kügelgen, *op. cit.*, p. 103.

[2] *Staatslexikon*, X, p. 751.

[3] *Ibid.*, p. 755.

[4] Quoted by Johann Jacoby, *Heinrich Simon*, Berlin, 1865, p. 221.

[5] *Germany: Revolution and Counter-Revolution* (Allen and Unwin edition, 8th impression, London, 1920), p. 11.

to foster a lively and responsible public opinion,[1] and three years later Robert Prutz attributed the fact that 'we have no parties' to the 'excessive fragmentation of opinion.'[2] When in 1841 Freiligrath declared that the poet should 'stand upon a higher watch-tower than the battlements of a party,'[3] Herwegh retorted that on the other hand the party was 'the mother of all victories.'[4]

This is the broad framework within which we have to consider the academic and scientific conferences. They were made possible by the growing self-consciousness and integration of the middle class. They served to advance its interests amid the class-struggles of the period, in which the campaign of the bourgeoisie was progressive in so far as it aimed at the establishment of a constitutional nation-state. In Great Britain and France parliaments already existed, but throughout the greater part of Germany 'there were still no forums of public discussion (Öffentlich-keit) in the full sense of the term—a sort of alternative had to be provided by associations and societies'[5]; as a popular history of the time remarked in the middle eighteen-forties, the very term 'society' (Verein) had 'become a slogan.'[6] In the absence of a developed parliamentary system they offered the intellectuals—the vanguard of the liberal movement—a substitute, to quote Gervinus, for 'the constitution, the assembly of the people, the forum, pub-licity' to which he attributed in English national life 'this healthy character and . . . this instinctive sureness of development.'[7] In conferences the intellectuals of the bourgeois movement could meet together from all parts of their divided country, not to sharpen existing differences, but to discover common ground. For, as Engels said

[1] Über den Begriff der politischen Partei, Königsberg, 1843.

[2] Zehn Jahre, Leipzig, 1850, p. 11.

[3] In the poem Aus Spanien.

[4] Gedichte eines Lebendigen.

[5] Valentin, Geschichte der Deutschen Revolution 1848–1849, Berlin, 1930, I, p. 89.

[6] K. W. Böttiger, Geschichte des deutschen Volkes und des deutschen Landes für Schule, Haus und für Gebildete überhaupt, Stuttgart, 1845, Pt. viii, p. 184.

[7] Die preussische Verfassung und das Patent vom 3. Februar, 1847, Mannheim, 1847, p. 104.

regarding the German bourgeoisie at this time, where there were no common interests there could be 'no unity of purpose, much less of action.'[1]

The academic and scientific conferences had a special significance from this point of view, but other gatherings require a brief mention. In 1817 large numbers of students and university teachers met together and founded the General German 'Burschenschaft.' The statutes of this organisation defined it as 'the free union of all German youth engaged in intellectual training at the universities for the developing unity of the German people.' The Hambach Festival of 1832, convened by the liberals and democrats of South Germany, had a similar national character. The celebrations in Leipzig in 1839 in honour of the fourth centenary of the invention of printing brought large numbers of the middle class together. Taken in conjunction with the agitation in favour of freedom of the press, it was, as Biedermann terms it, 'a popular and national festival in the fullest sense.'[2] The same was true of the Dürer celebrations in 1827 and of the Luther Festival, in which 'Turnvater' Jahn took part, in 1846, and of the liberal meeting at Offenbach in 1847. Jahn took a great delight in participating in all kinds of gatherings and, as his biographer says in words that are significant in this context, 'in the mere act of assembly he saw an element of patriotism.'[3] 'In the remembrance of the great men of their past,' it has been said, 'North and South Germans found points of contact in the feeling of unity that was beginning to inspire them, and in the activity of their intellectuals they found the central point to which their divergent forces strove.'[4]

The connection between the political movement of the bourgeoisie and the growth of societies appears in the attitude of the poet Uhland—who was also active in the liberal opposition in the Württemberg Diet and was later among the delegates to the Frankfurt National Assembly.

[1] *Op. cit.*, p. 12.

[2] *1840–1870. Dreissig Jahre deutscher Geschichte*, Breslau, 1896, I, p. 129.

[3] Heinrich Pröhle, *Friedrich Ludwig Jahns Leben*, Berlin, 1855, p. 255.

[4] Max von Boehn, *Biedermeier. Deutschland von 1815–1847*, 3rd ed., N/D, p. 312.

Eduard von Schenk, a Bavarian government official informed him of the plan to set up 'from above' and under princely protection a German Poets' Society. Uhland refused to take part. The symbol or the idea of unification, he said, was not enough. If Germans, he added, were once again called to arms, they would lack an essential weapon, the pride of the free citizen. Without the guarantee of democratic institutions the proposal offered stones instead of bread. 'If German poetry,' he commented, 'is to acquire a truly national vigour, its representatives cannot limit themselves to a historical or idyllic Germany. Each national question of the present day . . . must be able to be openly discussed.'[1] From a different point of view the connection is seen in the important Authors' Society in Leipzig in the eighteen-forties.[2] Not only did it draw large sections of the middle class together but, as Laube stressed, its business was conducted in such a way as to make it 'a training ground in parliamentary procedure.'[3]

It would be superfluous to mention all meetings and organisations which bear on these various aspects, but reference should be made to the Protestant Church Conference in Berlin in 1846. This event deserves special attention here because, as described in a contemporary essay,[4] it furnishes a valuable introduction to the conferences analysed in the following chapters.

Writing in the same year as the first of the two 'Germanisten' congresses, and like them influenced by the rising national feeling and in particular by the crisis in Schleswig-Holstein, the anonymous author of this document described recent tendencies in Germany thus: "Germany, although spiritually and physically separated in religion, ethos,

---

[1] Uhland's letter is printed in full in *Ludwig Uhlands Leben*. Aus dessen Nachlass und aus eigener Erinnerung zusammengestellt von seiner Wittwe, Stuttgart, 1874, pp. 289–94.

[2] In 1841 there was founded the '*Leipziger Litteratenverein*,' later called 'Deutscher Schriftstellerverein.' In 1845 it organised a conference of German writers in Leipzig, but the plan for a second such gathering was hindered by the government and could not take place till 1865. Cf. Heinrich Wuttke, *Die deutschen Zeitschriften und die Entstehung der öffentlichen Meinung*, Leipzig, 1875, pp. 67–8.

[3] *Erinnerungen, 1841–1881* (Baumüller ed.), p. 39.

[4] *Die kirchlichen Bewegungen in Deutschland und die protestantische Conferenz zu Berlin. Eine Stimme aus Schleswig-Holstein*, Schleswig, 1846.

dialects, customs, provinces and states, is now really only
divided as far as externals are concerned. All common
German interests both at home and abroad have been
especially emphasised and cultivated. Wherever the German national consciousness seemed damaged or threatened
. . . the effect has been felt throughout the whole of
Germany and discontent was loudly expressed. Similarly,
if anything of importance was taking shape in a single state
. . . its repercussions have been felt in the whole German
fatherland.'[1] It was, he continued, a consequence of this
situation that there came into existence 'societies comprising
men from all the German states . . . such as the annual
conferences of the German Scientists, Philologists and
Secondary Schoolmasters, Estate Managers and For-
esters . . .'[2] The Church Conference is 'a national German
undertaking.'[3] It 'is German . . . in its aims in the sense
that the purpose is to consult about common problems and
if possible to make a common decision,'[4] and 'even if
agreement cannot be reached, at any rate one of the objectives should be to draw people together.'[5] 'The feeling of
a firm sense of nationality,' he added, 'has reawakened and
Germany, in many ways outwardly divided, is conceived
. . . as a unity.'[6] These were very much the terms in
which people spoke of the academic and scientific conferences. Thus, asked by an outsider what was the purpose
of the 'Germanisten' congresses, one of their founders
answered: 'My wish is that we should learn to unite; wait
another hundred years and then we shall see what comes
of them.'[7]

It was only because these conferences succeeded in preserving the character of scholarly discussions that they were
able to get round the ban imposed by the German Confederation in 1832, as part of the campaign against the
liberal-national movement. This laid down: 'Extraordinary
popular gatherings and popular festivals, no matter under
what name and for what purposes, cannot . . . take place

[1] *Ibid.*, p. 31.   [2] *Ibid.*, p. 31.   [3] *Ibid.*, p. 35.

[4] *Ibid.*, p. 37.   [5] *Ibid.*, p. 38.   [6] *Ibid.*, p. 26.

[7] A. L. Reyscher, *Erinnerungen aus alter und neuer Zeit (1802 bis 1880)*,
Freiburg i. Br. and Tübingen, 1884, p. 100.

in any State of the Confederation without the prior consent
of the competent authority. Those who provide instigation
for such gatherings of festivals by verbal arrangement or
by circular are to be appropriately punished. Even in the
case of popular gatherings or festivals for which permission
has been granted, speeches of political content will not be
tolerated. . . . All societies which have political aims or
which are used for political purposes under other names
are to be forbidden in all the states of the Confederation
and fitting measures are to be taken against those who
participate in them.' In different localities there were often
regulations with a similar intention. The following ruling,
for example, applied to the universities in Baden: 'Those
who meet together for any public celebration. . . . or in
groups of more than four persons . . . as, for instance, a
reading-circle, must give notice of the fact to the university
office and request permission.'[1] How delicate a question
it was is seen from the experience of eight Berlin students
who in 1826 tried to form a society for the discussion of
problems of research. The scheme was vetoed by the government, which was so cautious in these matters that about
this time the only new organisation among students that it
was prepared to allow was a choral society, set up in 1827.[2]

Some of the most radical among the bourgeois intellectuals
of the time (Heine, Börne, Gutzkow, etc.), it is true, stood
aside from and sometimes in opposition to the universities.
Nevertheless the academic and scientific conferences are
extremely significant as showing, in a time of social change
and intellectual ferment, the ideas of important sections of
the intellectuals of the middle class. They are especially
valuable as focal points of thought under conditions when
in the different states there were wide divergences of circumstances and outlook.

If, for example, Mecklenburg offered a very unfavourable
basis for the growth of liberalism, the conditions in Baden
were for a variety of reasons far more auspicious. 'It is

---

[1] *Academische Gesetze für die Grossherzoglich Badischen hohen Schulen in
Heidelberg und Freiburg*, Karlsruhe, 1821.

[2] Cf. Max Lenz, *Geschichte der Königlichen Friedrich-Wilhelms-Universität zu Berlin*, Halle, 1910, II, 1, p. 183.

quite clear,' says Valentin, 'that the states of the south-west were felt as a politically homogeneous complex. . . . The politicians in Baden played a leading part in this respect and the will to be German was perhaps to be found there in its most lively form.'[1] However, even among these states there were important variations. Württemberg differed from the rest in that, for special reasons, the liberal struggle for democratic institutions centred more on the demand for the restoration of established prerogatives than on the agitation for new rights. In the Rhineland, where liberal-ism owed much to reforms imposed by Napoleon, to the relatively fast development of trade and to an economically favoured situation, the liberal intellectuals were much more closely associated with the commercial bourgeoisie than in most other parts. Another important centre of the liberal movement was Königsberg, but East Prussian liberalism had the special characteristic that the liberal middle class there was able to collaborate closely with an unusually liberal aristocracy—so much so that the rumour circulated that the Province was going to become independent with the popular President, Freiherr von Schön, as its king.[2] Apart from the differences in the various states, the focal points of liberalism were widely separated geographically. This fact was important in a period when rail communica-tions were either non-existent or only in an early stage of development.

The intellectual leaders of German liberalism in the first half of the century, moreover, were not always in full agreement as regards aim and method. They included, for example, Dahlmann, Gervinus, Welcker and Rotteck. The first, for a time Secretary of the Standing Deputation of the Prelates and Nobles of Holstein, became Professor of History at Kiel in 1813 and of Political Science at Göttingen in 1829. As one of the 'Göttingen Seven' he was dismissed in 1837. In 1842 he became a professor at Bonn, and in 1848 he was a prominent member of the Frankfurt National Assembly. Gervinus, a younger man, was also a member of this body and likewise among the

[1] *Op. cit.*, I, p. 162.
[2] Cf. Gustav Meyer, 'Die Anfänge des politischen Radikalismus im vormärzlichen Preussen,' in *Zeitschrift für Politik*, 1913, I, p. 23.

'Göttingen Seven'; he had been professor at Göttingen from 1836, transferring later to Heidelberg. Karl Theodor Welcker was Professor of Political Science at Freiburg from 1823 till his dismissal for political reasons in 1841; from 1831 he was a liberal member of the Second Chamber of the Baden Diet, and he too was in the Frankfurt National Assembly. He was closely associated with Rotteck, also professor at Freiburg (from 1832) and from 1819 likewise a member of the Baden Diet. There is much common ground between Dahlmann, a characteristic representative of the rightwing of the liberal movement, Gervinus, standing approximately at the centre, and Welcker and Rotteck, who were among the most prominent figures in the south-west. But, despite an early friendship, Dahlmann came to regard Welcker with distrust, considering him to be lacking in respect for the orderly development of society. Dahlmann's attitude[1] was summed up by Beseler thus: 'Above all, he has a basic hatred of everything that is revolutionary and, if he leans to one side, it is to that of the existing order.'[2] Such a generalisation would have been far less justified if applied to Welcker and Rotteck, though Häusser's view of them goes too far in the other direction. 'It is bad enough,' he wrote of the liberal opposition in Baden, 'that for a long time it participated in the sins of radicalism and operated with the sort of agitatorial methods that the radicals pursued with such virtuosity; it helped the guerilla warfare not only against the government but also against legality itself; it accustomed itself to that kind of political agitation which is more concerned to stir people up than to enlighten them.'[3] Even in Baden itself there was by no means uniformity among the liberal intellectuals. For example, there was considerable difference of emphasis between Welcker and Rotteck, despite their close collaboration in producing the celebrated *Political Lexikon*. Though Dahlmann suspected him of the sins of extremism, Welcker was in general

---

[1] Treitschke, in his essay (1864) on Dahlmann (in *Historische und politische Aufsätze*, I, Leipzig, 1886) sharply differentiates him from the more dogmatic liberalism of the south-west. Springer (in his two-volume biography, Leipzig, 1870–2) goes so far as to count him as a conservative.

[2] *Erlebtes und Erstrebtes, 1809–1859*, Berlin, 1884, p. 153.

[3] *Denkwürdigkeiten zur Geschichte der Badischen Revolution*, Heidelberg, 1851, pp. 59–60.

more cautious than Rotteck, more respectful of tradition.[1]

In the light of these considerations it can be understood that the academic conferences of the period met an obvious need. Welcker, for example, looking back on his own experience before 1848, spoke of 'the necessity for a lively interchange of ideas and for active propaganda on behalf of definite political tendencies with the aid of societies and gatherings,' which 'became more and more irresistible and general,' and he added: 'Here outside the Diets of the Estates was a training for the ability and exercise of impromptu speaking, for public debate and for parliamentary procedure.'[2] Gutzkow's remark that the conferences of the 'Germanisten' 'undoubtedly prepared the way for the Parliament in St. Paul's Church'[3] is valid in the same sense for the other conferences, and one recalls Riehl's statement that the debates of the 'Germanisten' 'have been correctly interpreted as the heralds of 1848.' 'A merely scholarly congress,' he adds, 'would not have had such importance if at the same time it had not been the form and expression of a social and political fact.'[4]

These conferences embody the attitude of the German intellectuals to a wide range of problems in these crucial stages of social and political struggle—to science, humanism, politics, history, language, law, etc. Not only do they indicate this attitude but they help to explain it. They throw valuable light on the development of the bourgeoisie in these years. Above all, they help us to follow the growth of German nationalism between its emergence as a defensive ideology under the stress of the Napoleonic invasion[5] and the point—already before 1848—when after an accumulation of quantitative changes it began to undergo the decisive qualitative transformation that set the pattern for the age of imperialism.

[1] Karl Wild, *Karl Theodor Welcker*, Heidelberg, 1913, is careful, and rightly so, to stress the features that differentiate Welcker's more moderate liberalism from Rotteck. Cf. also G. Hebeisen, *Die radikale und die konstitutionelle Partei in Baden* (Diss), Freiburg i. Br.

[2] From his article 'Verein,' in *Staatslexikon*, XIV, p. 355 seq.

[3] *Lebenserinnerungen*, in *Ausgewählte Werke* (ed. Houben), XI, p. 324.

[4] *Die bürgerliche Gesellschaft*, 8th ed., Stuttgart, 1885, p. 242.

[5] Cf. Roy Pascal, 'Nationalism and the German Intellectuals,' in *The German Mind and Outlook*, London, 1945.

CHAPTER I

THE CONFERENCES OF SCIENTISTS AND DOCTORS

In his account of the first of the conferences of Scientists and Doctors Lorenz Oken, their founder, raised the question why in England so many important works (dictionaries, encyclopaedias, etc.) had come into existence through the co-operation of scholars and 'why in Germany on the other hand virtually nothing of this kind develops.'[1]   The reason, he thought, was the different position of scholars in Germany from that in England or in France. 'In Germany,' he explained, 'we have no Paris or London; we have no place where hundreds of scientists and doctors live together.'[2] The conferences, which he organised, were to make good this deficiency in the national life of Germany. The society, in Schnabel's words, was to be 'a means of concentrating the German mind, of furthering the wishes of the nation and of preparing the way for political unification. . . . It was to be a centre of scholarship, such as France had in the Paris *Académie* and England in the Royal Society.'[3]

'If the home of French science,' it has been said, 'is to be found in the Académie,[4] that of German lay in the Universities.'[5] That the movement for German unity should have received significant and organised expression on a national scale for the first time in a body of people drawn from the universities, is itself significant. The explanation lies partly in the particularism of the small-state system, which made the development of centralised institutions impossible.   Moreover, it should be remembered that during the eighteenth century the German universities had begun to secure for themselves a measure of freedom which, in sharp contrast to the prevailing absolutism, was

[1] *Isis*, 1823, p. 553.   [2] *Ibid.*, 1823, p. 554.

[3] *Deutsche Geschichte im 19. Jahrhundert*, 1923, III, pp. 196–7.

[4] Académie des Sciences.

[5] W. C. Dampier, *A History of Science and Its Relations with Philosophy*, 3rd ed., Cambridge, 1942, p. 310.

formulated and cherished in the conception of the 'freedom of teaching and learning' (*Lern- und Lehrfreiheit*). By the first half of the nineteenth century university intellectuals in Germany were in a different position from other sections of the community. It is true that the universities were controlled by the individual states and to that extent were subject to the special conditions of particularism. But they drew their staff from other states as well, and so the professor or lecturer had to an exceptional extent the opportunity to move from one part of Germany to another. As Laube put it in his memoirs, "what was forbidden in Prussia was allowed in Baden; anyone who was evicted from one place took refuge in the neighbouring area."[1] The seven dismissed professors of Göttingen, for example, quickly found positions elsewhere. Thus the university teacher enjoyed certain advantages which were of particular value in the decades when the Carlsbad Decrees (1819) were in operation to bolster up the existing social and political structure. They formed, as it were, a mobile élite and to a striking degree they often felt themselves to be the bearers of the national idea, the conscience of the nation. The Prussian law of 1834 forbidding students to travel to other universities outside without prior permission underlines the importance of these considerations.

The novelty of the conferences of Scientists and Doctors did not consist in the fact that their main activity was the discussion of scientific problems or even that their meetings had political implications. There had been earlier organisations in Germany with these characteristics. There was, for example, the Natural Science Society in Jena, founded in 1793. Its primary purpose was scientific and its activities were coloured by political considerations—by fear of the Jacobin 'terror' and of subjection under a revolutionary France suspected of plans for universal domination.[2] References were made to 'German patriotism' but the whole character of the society was local rather than national. It never envisaged a 'German' basis as did the conferences of Scientists and Doctors. The same was true, for example,

[1] *Erinnerungen, 1810–1840* (Baumüller ed.), p. 140.
[2] Cf. *Nachricht von der Gründung einer naturforschenden Gesellschaft zu Jena am 14ten. Juli, 1793*, Jena, N/D, pp. 40–1.

of the Natural Science Society in Berlin even though, as Niebuhr mentioned[1] in his reply to a pamphlet of Schmalz,[2] Regnauld de St. Jean d'Angely reported in the wildest terms about its activities to the French Senate.

The fact that during the Napoleonic period considerable suspicions had been aroused by the existence of societies of this kind, some secret or semi-secret, called for tact on Oken's part in planning the conferences. After 1815, as we have seen, and especially after the Carlsbad Decrees, gatherings of almost any kind were viewed with suspicion in official circles. Oken's own record in the past did not make his task any easier.

Intensely devoted to the German cause, he was described by Jean Paul as 'a German to the core and in every turn of phrase.'[3] He was a scientist of importance, as Goethe recognised. 'Whether a person,' he said, 'shows himself to be a man of genius in learning like Oken and Humboldt or in war and political administration like Frederick or writes a song like Béranger, makes no difference. All that matters is whether the thought, the aperçu, the deed is vital and able to develop.'[4] Judged by this standard Oken's position in German history should be secure, not least through the success and influence of the society he founded.

He was born in 1779 in Baden of peasant stock. In 1800 he entered Freiburg University where he studied medicine, though he showed more interest in natural science and philosophy. After a period of further study at Würzburg he settled for the time being as lecturer at Göttingen. In 1807, in dire economic straits, he was invited to become Associate Professor at Jena, and it was here that he formulated his celebrated theory of the skull. He remained at Jena till 1819, the year of the Carlsbad Decrees. This was the most fruitful period of his life, in which some

[1] Cf. *Über geheime Verbindungen im preussischen Staat und deren Denunciation*, Berlin, 1815.

[2] *Berichtigung einer Stelle in der Bredow-Venturinischen Chronik für das Jahr 1808. Über politische Vereine und ein Wort über Scharnhorsts und meine Verhältnisse zu ihnen*, Berlin, 1815.

[3] Preface to 3rd ed. of *Hesperus*.

[4] To Eckermann, 11th March, 1828.

of his most important works were published. In 1816 he
founded the journal *Isis*. This appeared regularly till
1848 as an encyclopaedia of science and related subjects,
exercising a considerable influence both as a stimulus and
a meeting-ground of ideas; '*Isis* was indeed for a long time
a central organ of many branches of the natural sciences,
more so than any subsequent journal has been.'[1] In this
respect it was analogous to the conferences of Scientists and
Doctors. He was tactful enough formally to point out that
'it is not a political but a scientific journal. Only occasionally have political matters, so to say, strayed into it and
then against the will of the editor.'[2] By this time he had
developed an active interest in political and national
affairs. He had even gone so far as to set forth his ideas
in some detail about the military technique necessary for the
liberation of his country from Napoleon. 'Against the
enemy,' he wrote in 1814, in terms suggestive of the modern
'Blitzkrieg,' 'everything is permissible. It is ridiculous to
speak of the laws of war when one side aims at destroying
the other. . . . The insurrectionist can therefore use any
means he likes.'[3] He examined the same problem in another
short work, discussing even details of rifle construction and
the use of aerial balloons under siege conditions.[4] After
1815 he took an active part in the liberal-national movement
and in 1817 went to the Wartburg Festival. He reported
this event in *Isis* with the result that the number in question
was confiscated and publication had to be transferred to
Leipzig. As other serious difficulties arose for him largely
as a result of his share at this gathering, he decided to set
out on a journey to Munich and Paris. After lecturing for
a term at Basel he returned to Jena in 1822. He lived there
privately till 1827 when he accepted the chair of physiology
at Munich. Here too he encountered difficulties, partly
as a result of his share in a controversy regarding the place
of science in schools. On this subject he quarrelled with
Thiersch who, as will be seen, played much the same part

[1] *Allgemeine Deutsche Biographie*, XXIV, p. 217.

[2] *Isis*, 1817, p. 1297.

[3] *Überlegungen zu einer neuen Kriegskunst*, 1811.

[4] *Neue Bewaffnung, neues Frankreich, neues Deutschland*, 1814.

in the conferences of Classical Philologists, Secondary Schoolmasters and Orientalists as Oken in those of Scientists and Doctors. This argument led to Oken's resignation in 1832, but soon afterwards he was invited to a chair at Zürich, where he stayed till his death in 1851.

This outline will give some idea of the personality of the man, his energy and originality. His close connection with Jena should be noted. It was an important centre of the liberal-national movement before 1815 and remained so afterwards. In a divided Germany without a metropolitan centre it was important as one of the focal points of thought and activity. Its position was described from this point of view in 1843. 'Geographically and spiritually,' it was stated, 'Jena lies close to the heart of our nation. No other university is more sensitive to its pulse than ours. The university is also favoured by its political situation. Thuringia . . . is more divided than any other region of the country. Many princes rule here and the lands of each are divided. Thuringia is Germany in miniature. This fragmentation, which in other respects is certainly a great obstacle, has at any rate this advantage that, the smaller the community is, the better is the truly educated man able to keep his eye on the nation as a whole. This is the reason why in Thuringia there is more activity in societies and their organisation than in other states. Oken, the founder of the scientific conferences, came from Jena. . . . From the fragmentation of Thuringia the German nationalism of our university derives ever fresh nourishment.'[1]

As a thinker Oken's special field was Nature Philosophy. By modern standards he attached far too little importance to exact methods of analysis. The limitations of his thought are illustrated by his speculative attempt to demonstrate that everything is derived from 'nothingness.' Despite its speculative rather than analytical methods, however, Nature Philosophy in its best manifestations had the positive feature that it fixed attention on the intrinsic reality of natural phenomena. The notion of the polarity of forces in the process of change, conspicuous for example

---

[1] Fr. G. Schulze, *Über die Selbständigkeit des deutschen Universitätsgeistes mit besonderer Beziehung auf das Duell*, Jena, 1843, p. 12.

in the early work of Schelling, foreshadowed certain aspects of dialectical materialism. Thus Marx, writing to Feuerbach about Schelling in 1843, spoke of 'this sincere idea of the young Schelling, which remained for him just a youthful dream,' adding that 'Schelling is therefore a caricature of yourself in anticipation.'[1] Engels underlined this materialist aspect. 'It is perhaps easier,' he wrote in his foreword to the *Anti-Dühring*, 'to tear Nature Philosophy to bits with thoughtless vulgarity . . . than to appreciate its historical significance. It contains much that is nonsensical and fantastic, but no more than the unphilosophical natural scientists of the time. The fact that it also contains much sense and understanding is beginning to be realised since the theory of evolution has become more widely known. . . . The Nature Philosophers stand in the same relationship to consciously dialectical natural science as do the utopians to modern communism.'

Oken was a Nature Philosopher who became deeply convinced of the objective reality of nature and its laws. This attitude is seen, for instance, in his essay *On the Value of Natural History, Especially for the Education of Germans*. 'The return of philosophy,' he wrote in this work, 'to the object with which it occupied itself in the remote past, namely to nature, is an achievement of recent times, which for science holds out the promise of the same happy age that it enjoyed before ignorant sophistry and scholasticism displaced the natural sciences.' 'Nature Philosophy,'' he stated, 'has turned in a direction that is of a thoroughly material kind and which can only be continued by means of a rich and extensive knowledge of nature.' The relevance of these generalisations is not annulled by the fact that Oken was writing under the immediate impression of the Napoleonic invasion—'to work effectively we need insight into the necessity of material things, love of the stern discipline of natural science, devotion to the good cause— which is good because nature and dominant nations impose it on us.'

These considerations help towards a deeper understanding of Oken's connection with the conferences of Scientists and

[1] Marx-Engels, *Gesamtausgabe*, I, 2, p. 316.

Doctors in the general framework of the bourgeois movement and they throw light on the fact that the initiative for these came from a man intimately connected with Nature Philosophy. Some of the wider aspects can be indicated by reference to Hegel. The decline of the old order and the emergence and growth of the bourgeoisie was an underlying experience which stimulated his dialectical thinking and his application of it to the process of historical change. Moreover, his first significant advance towards a dialectical grasp of the problems confronting him as a thinker was made when he tackled questions of Nature Philosophy with a new insight and just before he began studying it with added energy in association with some of its exponents in Jena.[1]

These various factors suggest at least part of the answer to the question why it was the scientists who took the lead in organising academic conferences in these years. It was primarily material forces that made possible and stimulated the growth of the bourgeoisie; in the economic sphere all the advantages were on its side. The protagonists of the old order looked for their defence to less tangible features, such as the power of tradition and to ideological forces best calculated in the circumstances to sustain it. This was why the political struggle of the bourgeoisie involved attacks by its intellectuals on the fortress of orthodoxy. The attacks by Strauss on the historicity of Jesus,[2] and Feuerbach's attack on inspired religion[3] aroused so much bitterness and controversy because they appealed to the spirit of rational enquiry, thus endangering the defences of the existing state. 'If we can weaken people's faith,' declared Heine, 'we will make Germany a political force.'[4] When in the early eighteen-forties Marheineke, Professor of Theology at Berlin, had difficulties with the censor as a result of a mild criticism of the doctrine of revelation as applied philosophically by Schelling in his later period and when the students of Berlin demonstrated in Marheineke's favour, their action was fundamentally a political one.[5]

[1] Cf. Georg Lukacs, *Der junge Hegel*, Zürich, 1948, p. 276 seq.
[2] *Das Leben Jesu*, 1835.   [3] *Das Wesen des Christentums*, 1841.
[4] Quoted in A. J. P. Taylor (ed.), *The Opening of an Era: 1848*, London, 1948, p. 22.
[5] For an account of this episode cf. Willibald Beyschlag, *op. cit.*, pp. 139–40.

In the same way the 'Lichtfreunde' movement—a Protestant revolt against the dogmatic pietism fostered, after some brief concessions to liberalism, by Frederick William IV soon after his accession in 1840—had far-reaching implications. It is noteworthy that Willibald Beyschlag, a liberal clergyman, while disliking the rationalist theology of the 'Lichtfreunde,' was inclined to be sympathetic to them in their attitude to the Prussian king. 'It was only natural,' he wrote, 'that the "Lichtfreunde" drew together in common defence, and that far and wide, also outside Prussia, the sympathy of the Protestant bourgeoisie was aroused in their support; people felt themselves summoned from within Prussia to a war in the defence of the Protestant freedom of thought and faith.'[1] The political implications of the religious controversies at this time are mirrored in a statement of Laube who, describing his attitude to events, spoke of his search for 'a deeper content of life which I termed political religion.'[2] Beyschlag saw the situation clearly when, discussing the 'Lichtfreunde,' he said: 'The long repressed craving in Germany for public institutions and public debate seemed in the last resort to turn to the church questions of the time and so to exercise itself in preparation for 1848.'[3] 'The agitation for a freer organisation of church life,' wrote Haym in a similar connection, 'served at the same time to prepare the ground for participation in public affairs as a whole. Liberalism in the church was the training school for political liberalism.'[4] Writing to Feuerbach in 1843, Ruge declared: 'Theology is for Germany the only practical and successful vehicle for politics, at any rate for the moment.'[5]

Already before the attacks had begun in earnest on the stronghold of religious orthodoxy a similar trend was evident in the scientific field towards the appeal to rational analysis and scientific observation. Important in this

---

[1] *Ibid.*, pp. 256–7.

[2] *Erinnerungen, 1810–40* (Baumüller ed.), p. 156.

[3] *Op. cit.*, p. 255.

[4] *Aus meinem Leben*, Berlin, 1902, p. 167.

[5] *Arnold Ruges Briefwechsel und Tagebuchblätter aus den Jahren 1825–1880*, ed. Paul Nerrlich, Berlin, 1886, I, p. 304.

connection was the mathematical work of Gauss[1] and the
chemical research of Liebig[2] who, after studying in Paris
under Gay-Lussac, opened a laboratory in Giessen in 1826.
This tendency, as we shall see, had its counterpart in legal,
political and historical thought. It was an important
element in the growth of German liberalism which was
'impossible without the simultaneous growth of empirical
science, both went hand in hand.'[3]

One of the most important figures in Germany in this
connection was Alexander von Humboldt. After living
for some time in the freer social and intellectual atmosphere
of Paris he returned to Berlin in 1827, some twenty years
after he had disappointed the hope that he might become
one of the early glories of his brother's creation, the University of Berlin. For the winter of 1827 Humboldt, now a
celebrity of European scholarship, announced a course of
lectures at the university on physical geography. These
drew an immense audience from wide sections of Berlin
society, including the King of Prussia, and from them
emerged his most famous work *Cosmos* (1845–58). 'But
the importance of these lectures,' it has been said, 'goes
further than this. They proclaimed a new age. They were
a protest against the excesses of speculation. . . . They
raised, as Alfred Dove says, "empirical science . . . on to
the spiritual throne of the time" . . .' As the same
writer points out, it is strange that these lectures should
have been held under royal patronage in view of the fact
'that empirical science, accounts of the world and the study
of its history, more than any speculation, undermined the
foundations on which the old outlook rested.'[4]

The conflict between the two points of view was particularly sharp in the eighteen-forties. Among the leading

---

[1] Professor and Director of the Observatory at Göttingen from 1807.
His works included *Disquisitiones arithmeticae* (1801), *Theoria motus
corporum coelestium* (1809), *Dioptrische Untersuchungen* (1841).

[2] Professor at Giessen, 1824–52, and thereafter at Munich. For a brief
account, partly in Liebig's own words, of his experiences in Paris, where he
was greatly stimulated by the "practical' character of French science in
contrast to the 'predominance of the deductive method' of German
scientists, cf. Theodor Heuss, *Justus von Liebig*, Hamburg, 1949, p. 10 seq.

[3] Schnabel, *op. cit.*, II, pp. 195–6.

[4] Lenz, *op. cit.*, p. 362 seq.

figures in this respect was Jakob Henle. As a young man he had been active in the liberal-nationalist 'Burschenschaft' at Bonn, thereby securing for himself with the authorities a reputation which, but for the intervention of Alexander von Humboldt, might have ended his academic career.[1] In 1844 Henle and Karl von Pfeuffer, one of his colleagues, left Zurich for Heidelberg. Towards the end of their time in Zurich they had formed a close friendship based on identity of outlook on politics and philosophy and they had collaborated in editing a periodical entitled *Journal for Rational Medicine*. The first number contained a manifesto by Henle with the significant title 'On Medical Science and Empiricism.' 'Medicine at that time,' wrote a contemporary doctor, 'was only just beginning consciously to free itself from the bonds of Nature Philosophy and of blind faith and superstition. There was still a large number of doctors who held that medicine could be systematically deduced from a general principle. In Bavaria science and art had to subordinate themselves to theosophy; the all-powerful Medical Superintendent Ringeis, who exercised an often decisive influence there on appointments to medical posts and professorships, deduced disease from the Fall and tried to cure it with the means of grace offered by the church.'[2]

The experience of Henle provides a useful illustration of the connection between these antagonisms, between speculation and empiricism, and the political trends. 'One can understand,' says the same writer, regarding the political aspects of Henle's manifesto, 'that in the period just before 1848 medical students, who were filled with a spirit of progress and were in combative mood, welcomed the swish of the whips which the important anatomist swung over the heads of the obscurantists.'[3] At Heidelberg Henle and Pfeuffer soon found a circle of men sympathetic to their ideas. These included, outside the medical faculty, Gervinus

---

[1] Henle's romantic marriage was used by Auerbach in his novel *Die Frau Professorin* (1846) and by Charlotte Birch-Pfeiffer (1800–68) in her play *Dorf und Staat*.

[2] Adolf Kussmaul, *Jugenderinnerungen eines alten Arztes*, 2nd ed., Stuttgart, 1899, pp. 237–8.

[3] *Ibid.*, p. 238.

and other liberal intellectuals. When the events of 1848 opened the doors to reaction, Henle transferred to Göttingen, Pfeuffer to Munich.

These reflections on the relationship between certain spiritual and intellectual trends and the political struggles of the age help us to see the conferences of Scientists and Doctors in their full perspective.

It was from Switzerland that Oken derived the idea of organising the conferences. In 1815 there took place in Geneva the first discussion about the possibility of founding a Swiss scientific society. The plan was that it should be a 'Wandergesellschaft,' i.e. a society meeting annually in a different town. It held its first meeting in Berne. Oken was extremely interested in the scheme, discussed it in *Isis*, attended its congress at Zurich in 1817 and set about examining the opportunities for a similar venture in Germany. He met with no success in his contacts with existing bodies and so decided to tackle the problem in a different way. He communicated his intention to wide circles with a view to creating a new and independent organisation.

Oken was certainly optimistic in the circumstances in hoping for widespread support at the beginning. Particularly in academic circles his proposal met with considerable misgivings. From the University of Bonn, for instance, he received a letter expressing all manner of doubts, fears and objections. Oken's comment was characteristically frank. 'In this letter,' he said scornfully, 'one sees the German from every possible angle—one sees him from the front and from the back, from below and from above. Misgivings are stated about the cost, misgivings about the journey, misgivings about the faces of the people, misgivings about the accommodation, misgivings about the knowledge required, misgivings about the room and finally misgivings about the reaction of the governments!'[1] German scholars were for the most part too limited in their political horizon, too much the victims of the parochialism of the small-state system and of Germany's social, economic and political backwardness to be able to view Oken's ambitious and

[1] Quoted by Südhoff, *Hundert Jahre deutscher Naturforscher-Versammlungen*, Leipzig, 1922, p. 5.

imaginative project with equanimity. At the first meeting, for example, many of those present refused to allow their names to be recorded because of the fear that, if discovered, it might arouse the ire of their rulers.[1] The reception given to Oken's suggestion was described by Carus. 'Oken's proclamation,' he wrote, 'was regarded by most of the professors at Leipzig merely as an eccentric idea and only few people in other places had recognised its significance.'[2]

The inaugural conference was held in 1822 in humble quarters in Leipzig. It was hardly an auspicious year in which to make a beginning, for in April a Cabinet Order in Prussia was issued forbidding university teachers to discuss political questions of the moment under pain of dismissal. It is true that Oken had never suggested that there were to be political discussions, but the governments tended to interpret the term 'political' rather arbitrarily, especially following the Carlsbad Decrees. In any case, in the particular circumstances of the time there was always the danger that debates might become involved in politics, even unintentionally. Though the instigation came from Oken, others joined him in sponsoring the new venture. Numerically the opening conference was disappointing; only about twenty members attended. But a start had been made and the numbers were to rise with surprising rapidity.

In order to qualify as a member a person was required, in accordance with section 3 of the statutes, to have published a work on science or medicine, not including doctoral dissertations. At the first meeting, in addition to the members, some sixty guests were present.[3] The practice of allowing guests to attend the meetings was to remain an important feature of the organisation. It was stated in the statutes (section 9) as a principle that the conferences were to be public. In 1826, for example, there were one hundred and fifty members to some two hundred and fifty guests. In 1847 the number of members had risen to six hundred and fifty. The meeting in 1842 at Mainz was exceptional in

[1] Cf. *ibid.*, p. 10.

[2] *Lebenserinnerungen und Denkwürdigkeiten*, Leipzig, 1865–6, II, p. 182.

[3] Cf. *Allgemeine Literatur-Zeitung*, November, 1822.

that nearly a thousand people attended. The decision to admit interested people as guests was part of a deliberate policy of giving the greatest possible publicity to the discussions. They were lifted out of the narrowly academic sphere, constituting something in the nature of a forum of debate and public opinion, such as the liberal intellectuals felt to be vital to their cause.

It was one thing to state this as an ideal, another to achieve it in practice. The main difficulty was that German scholars were for the most part unaccustomed to address themselves to wider audiences consisting not merely of specialists. This deficiency reflected the narrowness of German middle class life up to this time, the lack of political consciousness and ambition among the bourgeoisie. The desire to overcome it can only properly be understood in the light of the social and economic changes influencing the intellectual vanguard of the bourgeoisie in these years, concentrating its efforts, and stimulating its class-consciousness and its desire to clarify and popularise its outlook. Oken saw further than many of his contemporaries in Germany when he stressed the need for scholars to learn to speak easily and attractively. This was why at the second conference the proposal was made, at Oken's instigation, that members should adopt 'lively and impromptu delivery in place of the painful reading aloud of written texts.'[1] The plan broke down, however, 'because German scholars were still the slaves of their manuscripts,'[2] but the member who in 1832 addressed the conference in Latin is interesting only as a curiosity.

The fact that Oken recognised the problem and tried to tackle it in this way illustrates the importance of considering the academic and scientific conferences as a training ground of the intellectuals of the liberal middle class for the political struggle that was to culminate in 1848. Oken's emphasis on the need for the intellectuals to learn to communicate their ideas in order to render them effective has a close parallel, as will be seen in connection with the 'Germanisten,' in the attitude of those liberal historians of the time who said that history should be written in a more popular style

[1] Südhoff, op. cit., p. 20.   [2] Ibid., p. 20.

in order that it might more usefully serve as a weapon
in the political arena. One is reminded too of the efforts
of the group of Young German writers in the eighteen-
thirties to secure acceptance of their ideas among a broad
public by writing in a popular, often journalistic, manner.
Another comparison, from the century of the English
bourgeois revolution, is with the Royal Society. 'There is
one thing more,' Bishop Spratt wrote in the first history of
the Society, 'about which the Society has been most
sollicitous; and that is, the manner of their Discourse:
which, unless they had been very watchful to keep in due
temper, the whole spirit and vigour of their Design, had been
soon eaten out by the luxury and redundancy of speech.'
He comments: 'They exacted from their members a close,
naked, natural way of speaking; positive expressions, clear
senses; a native easiness; bringing all things as near the
Mathematical Plainness, as they can: and preferring the
language of Artisans, Countrymen and merchants, before
that of Wits and Scholars.'[1] As Basil Willey says, 'no
clearer proclamation could be desired of the victory of the
new world-picture, the fact-world, over the old worlds of
traditional feeling.'[2]

It would be the task of a scientist to assess the technical
significance of the debates at these conferences. Goethe
was not impressed by it. 'Dear old Germany,' he wrote
to Zelter in July, 1828, 'has strange things to show in her
own way. I have been on the lookout to see whether in
the scientific conferences . . . there was anything that
affected, provoked, stimulated me, who for the last fifty
years has been passionately devoted to science. But,
apart from certain details, which in any case only gave me
a bit of information, I got nothing from them; no new
demand was made on me, no new gift proffered.'[3] The
strictly scientific features need not much concern us, for
the main importance of the conferences did not lie in details
of scientific debate but in broader aspects.

[1] *History of the Royal Society*, 2nd ed., 1702, p. 111.

[2] *The Seventeenth Century Background*, 4th impression, London, 1949,
p. 213.

[3] Quoted by Frédéric Soret, *Zehn Jahre bei Goethe, Erinnerungen an
Weimars klassische Zeit, 1822–1832*, Leipzig, 1929, p. 247.

Not the least significant of these was the social and recreational side of the activities. This was regarded as so vital that at the 1841 conference at Brunswick members felt obliged to defend themselves against Oken's charge that they were not concentrating sufficiently on being distracted. It might be tempting to treat this feature with tolerant ridicule. But it must be remembered that the other academic conferences of the period gave it an equally prominent place in their meetings. 'The over-industrious scholars,' it was said of Germany in the eighteenth century, 'see other people so little that, as far as social life is concerned, they always remain a sort of semi-savage. It is almost true to say that the major part of university teachers consists of men whom one could not take out of their own circle into mixed company without their provoking a smile.'[1] This corresponds to another comment by a writer in the first years of the nineteenth century. He observed that most university teachers came from poor circumstances with the result 'that they are incapable of doing anything outside their learned works, that the most famous men behave in ordinary life like children or people from the lowest sections of society, that in the company of others— especially with the great—they appear like the inhabitants of a different world and thereby cause themselves to be treated with contempt or scant respect.'[2] This description had a basis in fact, even though it was a caricature in many individual cases. At any rate, it was a far-cry to the prestige enjoyed, for example, both as a scholar and a man of the world by Alexander von Humboldt. His lectures in Berlin were social occasions, officers and privy councillors sitting among the students in the packed auditorium.[3] Apart from increased salaries,[4] the change was due to the heightened economic and social status of the bourgeoisie

[1] Quoted by Emil Reicke, *Der Gelehrte in der deutschen Vergangenheit*, Leipzig, 1900, p. 142.

[2] Meiners, *Geschichte der Entstehung und Entwicklung der hohen Schulen unseres Erdteils*, Göttingen, 1802–5, II, p. 10 seq.

[3] This is not to suggest that the type of isolated and unworldly intellectual had disappeared. Cf. for example, Tieck's amusing story *Der Gelehrte* (1827)—which provided Freytag with the prototype for the hero of his novel *Die verlorene Handschrift*.

[4] For some details of academic salaries, etc., in the eighteenth century cf. Reicke, *op. cit.*, p. 143 seq.

side by side with the relative decline of the aristocracy.[1]

The social consequence of these developments was a tendency, mirroring on a small scale trends in the bourgeoisie as a whole, for its intellectuals to draw closer together. If in the eighteenth century their relationships had been marked by petty strife and jealousy, increasing co-operation and mutual respect were evident in the nineteenth. In this period university professors came to think of themselves less as a closed guild and more as members of a broader social unit. In 1819, for instance, Rotteck impatiently rejected the idea[2] that there should be such a thing as a 'scholars' estate,' when he took issue with an argument of the Kantian philosopher Fries that a 'Gelehrtenstand' was a necessary part of any government by estates. The fact that Scientists and Doctors could meet together year by year, that Classical Philologists could join hands with Secondary Schoolmasters and Orientalists, that university teachers of German Law, German Philology and German History could jointly discuss common problems, that each group of conferences could openly acknowledge its debt to others, that in these conferences co-operative enterprises in the field of scholarship could be proposed and to some extent carried out—these features reflected a social development within the bourgeoisie of the utmost importance. It is nevertheless true that verbal battles in the learned journals continued to be unnecessarily bitter; Oken, for example, felt it necessary to stress the need 'of introducing a decent and gentler tone into the mutual judgments of one scholar by another.'[3] Moreover, there were not lacking men like Mittermaier, who campaigned for a title on the grounds that he was sick of standing among his colleagues 'like a poor sheep as a mere professor.'[4]

This background indicates the significance of section 2 of the statutes of these conferences, in which it was laid

[1] Cf. Friedrich Paulsen, *Die deutschen Universitäten und Universitätsstudium*, Berlin, 1902, p. 234.

[2] Cf. *Ideen über Landstände*, Karlsruhe, 1819, p. 49, in connection with Fries' *Von deutschem Bund und deutscher Staatsverfassung*, Heidelberg, 1816.

[3] *Isis*, 1823, p. 555.

[4] Quoted by Friedrich von Bezold, *Geschichte der Rheinischen Friedrich-Wilhelms-Universität*, Bonn, 1920–33, I, p. 193.

down: 'The main aim of the Society is to give the Scientists and Doctors of Germany the opportunity to get to know each other.' This feature was underlined by Humboldt at the 1828 meeting: 'The principal purpose of the Society . . .' he said, 'unlike other academies which form a closed unit, does not consist in the mutual exchange of treatises, in numerous lectures, all of which are destined to be printed and which will appear more than a year later in special collections. The principal purpose of this Society is the personal rapprochement of men who work in the same field of knowledge; the oral and therefore more stimulating exchange of ideas, whether as facts, opinions or doubts; the formation of friendly relations which impart light to scholarship, grace to life, and tolerance and gentleness to manners.'[1]

The social activities were, in fact, regarded as so important that they were regularly recorded in the published proceedings. At the Hamburg conference, for instance, one of the most successful events was an excursion to Heligoland, in honour of which occasion Lappenberg (later one of the founders of the 'Germanisten' conferences) wrote his pamphlet *On the Earlier Size and History of the Island of Heligoland* (1830). The report mentions that on the way members admired 'the sight of the infinite sea and the many vessels crossing it in all directions.'[2] From the account, the pathos of which strikes us to-day as rather amusing, it is clear that the experience made a deep impression on those present, many of whom had seen little of Germany and its surroundings outside their own locality. On Heligoland these learned gentlemen were sufficiently roused from their academic privacy as to dance with what the report describes with feeling as 'the fine, natural and blooming girls of the island in merry mood.'[3] But we are assured that, while also admiring the cheapness and high quality of food and drink, they did not fail to devote themselves at the same

---

[1] *Amtlicher Bericht über die Versammlungen deutscher Naturforscher und Ärzte zu Berlin im September, 1828*, Berlin, 1829, p. 15. This was the first conference of which official 'Proceedings' were published. Thereafter they appeared regularly—as a rule, published the following year at the place of the conference. Before 1828 we have to rely on short summaries in *Isis*.

[2] *Ibid.*, 1830, p. 57.   [3] *Ibid.*, 1830, p. 57.

time to the more serious tasks of scientific observation. The lighter side of the activities at the Hamburg conference are described by a doctor who took part in them. 'The pleasures,' he wrote, 'of the scientific conference at Hamburg included the meetings in the evening in the Apollo Hall, where the older people could chat and the younger dance. The Lady Mayoress, Frau Bartels . . . and her daughter . . . an imposing blonde, did the honours.'[1] The tone of the account reflects the light-hearted spirit of the occasion.

An important feature of the social activities were the organised meals at which members were asked to be present. The method of organisation was determined by their purpose, which was to bring members into personal contact with each other. Thus, at the conference at Berlin a scholar from Berlin sat at each table. His place was fixed, but the rest of the company were encouraged to change their seats on the different occasions. In 1829 instructions were issued urging everyone to participate in the official meals 'in order that the short time of the meeting may be of the greatest possible pleasure and value.'[2]

It is true that there were individuals who looked down with supercilious amusement at this aspect of the conferences. Some, like Alexander von Humboldt, vacillated between praise and disapproval. In 1829 he wrote to the French scientist Geoffroy Saint-Hilaire as follows: 'The inestimable advantage of this organisation is the contact between so many scholars from Germany, Sweden, Denmark, Holland, the possibility of discussing in three weeks[3] what would have to be sought in the course of long journies. . . . These specialist sections or gatherings were of the greatest interest at Berlin and left their mark not only on the writings but also on the spirit of those who understand the art of discussion and do not carry with them a deplorable despotism into the search for truth. Public opinion forms itself and attention is fixed on people whose names were unknown

[1] Stromeyer, *Erinnerungen eines deutschen Arztes*, Hannover, 1875, II, p. 25. Stromeyer ended his career as Director of Medical Services to the Hannoverian army. He died in 1876.

[2] *Amtlicher Bericht*, 1829, p. 10.

[3] The meetings did not last three weeks. Presumably Humboldt includes the time spent on the journey.

until then.'[1] But his comments were not always so favourable. In 1832 he explained in a letter that, in order not to interrupt his work, he had not attended the Vienna meeting 'where . . . the vanity of the learned found satisfaction in various ways.'[2] In 1837, in a letter to Gauss, he said that he preferred his company to that of all the scientists 'who move about in such huge masses and with such gastronomical enthusiasm that for my part there was not enough scientific discussion.'[3]

Stromeyer, whose reminiscences have already been quoted, summed up the situation realistically when he wrote as follows: 'Scientists and Doctors knew each other very little as yet and in the gatherings they met on neutral ground. An occasional meeting commits one to nothing, unlike say a visit to somebody's house, which can be interpreted as a concession through which one enters, as it were, into the relationship of a vassal. Once people have seen each other at a Scientific Conference they can then fight and hate each other to their hearts' content. If one wished to raise the status of these gatherings, which have rather declined in prestige, one would only have to interrupt them for ten years. The desire to get to know one another would gain the upper hand, the leaders of science would no longer be so conceited and so indifferent to the wishes of their admirers who wished to see and hear them again after having long read about the famous men.'[4] Finally, Goethe's comment deserves to be recorded. In 1830 he spoke thus to Eckermann: 'I know perfectly well that in these conferences not so much emerges for science as one might think; but they are excellent for the reason that people get to know each other. From this follows that one will be willing to accept some new doctrine of an important person and he in turn will be inclined to recognise and help us in our line in a different subject. At any rate, we see that something is happening and no one can know what will come of it.'[5]

---

[1] Quoted by Karl Bruhns, *Alexander von Humboldt*, Leipzig, 1872, II, pp. 167–8.

[2] Quoted in *ibid.*, p. 169.   [3] Quoted in *ibid.*, p. 169.

[4] *Op. cit.*, II, p. 25.   [5] To Eckermann, 27th January, 1830.

It is easy, in following the details of organisation and activity, to forget that it is only in the broader political perspectives that the full significance of the conferences can be properly understood.   To take another example, section 8 of the statutes laid down that 'everything must be settled by a majority vote.'   For many intellectuals of the time it was a big step from traditional habits to the idea of collaboration in an assembly which decided its issues in this way.   It signified a departure from the conception of the scholar as a mere individual responsible only to the voice of his own conscience.   It was a valuable schooling for political struggle.

An important practical question, affecting this aspect of the conferences, was whether or not all the sessions were to be of a general kind—in other words, whether the creation of specialist sections should be allowed.   There was clearly a danger that specialist activities might come to play such a preponderant part as to disrupt the corporate character, which it was Oken's main aim to foster.   He was consulted and gave what was obviously wise advice.   His view was that sections should be permitted but that there should always be a fixed number of occasions when all members of the conference met in general session.   This was the official policy, though in the course of time various modifications and alternatives were proposed.   It did not prove easy to preserve the balance.   Thus, when the Society sent Oken an invitation to attend the meeting at Aix-la-Chapelle in 1847,[1] it enclosed a copy of a report drawn up by a committee set up to review the position.   One of his main comments on this document was that the organisation was tending to degenerate into sections, and he urged the need to preserve the importance of the three general sessions.

Another suggestion as to the means of maintaining the unity of the conferences was that members should collaborate in research and compilation.   Oken was fully in agreement about the value of such work from this point of view.   At the first conference Froriep, who had been planning a

---

[1] Oken had attended all conferences till 1830, but thereafter he went only to those at Stuttgart (1834) and Freiburg (1838).   One of the reasons he gave for his absence was his dislike of public acclamation, but there were hints of friction.

German naturalist dictionary, was asked to submit specimens of this in order to see whether it was worth pursuing on a co-operative basis. At the conference in 1840 a plan, already mooted, was discussed for the preparation of a German encyclopaedia of medicine, but without concrete results. At Mainz in 1842 the conference sympathetically considered a copy of a memorandum sent by the Director of the Apothecaries Society of the Palatinate to the King of Bavaria on the 'need for a general German pharmacopoeia.' Though little matured from beginnings such as these, they had their significance as betokening a desire among these scholars to collaborate in the production of large-scale works of a national kind, and they had their parallel, as will be seen, in the other conferences.

Oken's opinion had also been asked as to whether the organisation could not achieve greater integration by establishing a central headquarters. To this idea he was absolutely opposed. From the start his plan was that it should meet annually in a different place, like the Swiss 'Wandergesellschaft' on which it was modelled. It was stated in the statutes that the conference should always be held in a town within the German Confederation; a proposal at Heidelberg in 1829 to extend these limits to other German-speaking areas was turned down. Oken recommended that, generally speaking, the aim should be to choose towns with a university or the residence of a prince, on the grounds that such places were likely to offer the best facilities, and this was the usual practice. This was one of the most characteristic and influential features and it was adopted by the other conferences. It had many advantages, all connected with Oken's conception of the meetings as 'the spiritual symbol of the unity of the German people.'[1] It enabled a greater number of scholars to take part, at any rate on occasions; travel was not yet sufficiently easy for people to go far away from home year after year without serious cost and inconvenience. It also gave the maximum publicity to the Society. It took people out of the confines of the state in which they lived, familiarised them with other regions of their country and helped thus

[1] Quoted by Südhoff, op. cit., p. 32.

to arouse in them the consciousness of a common fatherland. Moreover, it brought the conferences into touch with a large number of local and regional societies. These would establish contact with the Scientists and Doctors when they visited their district, thus giving the conferences something of the character of a rallying-point of scientific study independent of the political barriers within a divided country. This is what Südhoff had in mind when he said that by the eighteen-forties the 'increasingly cordial linking-up' enhanced its importance as 'a mobile focal point' in the world of German science. Contacts were also established between these conferences and others in different fields, for example, with that of the Philosophers in 1846[1] and with the congresses of the Estate and Forest Managers, which, inspired by the Scientists and Doctors and influenced by their form of organisation, came into existence in 1837.[2]

The theme of German unity was heard again and again in the discussions of the Scientists and Doctors. At Berlin in 1828 it was conspicuous in the speech of Alexander von Humboldt. He interpreted his election as Secretary, he said, to the fact that after his long absence abroad people wanted 'to bind me longer and more tightly to our common fatherland,' and he proceeded to describe the gathering as an assembly of men from all the different parts of Germany united in their determination 'to penetrate the secret processes of nature.'[3] Though he also spoke about this meeting in less flattering terms—he wrote to Decandolle about this 'irruption of scholars that makes one tremble' and described it to Derichelet as 'this literary fair'[4]—he added (in the letter to Derichelet): 'But it has a serious side, for it is a noble manifestation of the unity of German scholarship. It is the nation divided in beliefs and in politics that reveals itself to itself in its intellectual powers.' A speaker at Kiel talked of 'the idea of the united fatherland which is now inseparably bound up with our conferences.'[5]

[1] Cf. p. 66.

[2] The title of this body was 'Versammlung deutscher Land-und Forst-wirte.' Its *Amtlicher Bericht* was published annually.

[3] *Amtlicher Bericht*, 1828, p. 14.

[4] Quoted by Bruhns, *op. cit.*, II, p. 157.

[5] Quoted by Südhoff, *op. cit.*, p. 32.

'It is splendid,' said a speaker at Heidelberg, 'to see gathered together from all the German states men who demonstrate the completest harmony and their common interests, or with the lack of which our nation has for centuries been reproached.'[1] 'From now on,' exclaimed a member at Vienna, 'north and south are merged together. A single bond unites us all and there is no separation between us on German soil. O my dear and adored fatherland, how much would I like, before I die, to see you once again great and glorious as in the times of our fathers, great and strong through the unity and love of all thy children!'[2]

Such ideas, harmless as they appear, were always liable to arouse the displeasure of the governments, but it was when the Scientists and Doctors met for the first time in the Prussian capital in 1828 that the greatest circumspection was necessary. Indeed, it is doubtful whether the Berlin meeting could have taken place at all but for Humboldt's prestige and authority both at court and among a wider public. It was, for example, only as a result of his pleading that members were released on arrival at Berlin from the irritating and humiliating necessity of presenting themselves at the office at which visitors were normally required to register; in return, he undertook to send a daily list of arrivals to the police. The authorities had misgivings not only about the possible implications of such a scientific organisation but also as regards Oken himself in view of his political activities in the past. The prospect of welcoming Oken at Berlin as the principal figure in the conference caused anxiety. The king, however, was persuaded by Humboldt as to the innocuous character of the organisation, with the astonishing result that Oken appeared arm in arm with Kamptz, the police chief of Prussia, 1817–25, the arch-enemy of liberalism and one of the leading organisers of its suppression after the Carlsbad Decrees. Oken was always as careful as possible to prevent incidents likely to awaken the hostility of the authorities, and more than ever so on this important occasion. One example is worth mentioning, because it has a bearing on an important aspect

---

[1] *Amtlicher Bericht*, 1829, p. 12.

[2] Quoted by Südhoff, *op. cit.*, pp. 27–8.

discussed earlier in this chapter. The proposal was made to form a psychological section. Oken's reactions are described by a scholar who was present. 'Oken protested most seriously,' he said, 'against our intention. His reason was that in discussions of a psychological-scientific kind views would be expressed which would conflict with religious dogma and might make the conferences suspect to governments.'[1]

Alexander von Humboldt showed himself as always a master of discretion. His address was delivered in the presence of the Crown Prince and the Duke of Cumberland. He emphasised the national consciousness of the scholars gathered in Berlin, but he was wise enough to combine this with an affirmation of civic duty and in the same context to mention some of the advantages that might be claimed for particularism. 'Under the protection of noble princes,' he declared, 'the interest and scope of this Society have grown year by year. Every difference which might be created by divergence of religion or constitution is here resolved. Germany reveals itself in its spiritual unity.' But he went on: 'Just as the recognition of the truth and the performance of duty is the highest purpose of morality, this feeling of unity does not weaken any of the bonds which make religion, the constitution and the laws of our home state dear to us. It is precisely the differentiated life of the German nation, this rivalry in the realm of the spirit that produced, as the glorious history of our country shows, the fairest flowers of humanity, scholarship and art.'[2]

These various aspects indicate in their different ways the relationship between the conferences of Scientists and Doctors and the rise of continental liberalism. Their importance from this point of view becomes even clearer if it is borne in mind that they had a striking parallel in another part of Europe.

Italy at this time resembled Germany in so far as it too was a territorially and politically divided nation in which the bourgeoisie took the lead in the struggle for unification and parliamentary democracy. The scientific conferences,

[1] K. F. Burdach, *Rückblick auf mein Leben*, Leipzig, 1848, p. 383.

[2] *Amtlicher Bericht*, 1828, p. 14.

which came into existence there in the same period, played a role similar to those in Germany as part of the prelude to a bourgeois revolution. A speaker at one of these conferences went straight to the point when he said that he craved 'to drive a knife through the hearts of those that would not build Italian unity.'

In 1831 the literary review *Antologia*, founded by the Florentine liberals in 1820, published an article—reprinted in the Lombard liberal journal *Annali*—advocating a national congress of Italian scientists. This idea took practical shape in 1839 when the first of a series of conferences was held at Pisa under the patronage of Leopold II of Tuscany. The founders included Carlo Bonaparte, son of Napoleon's brother Lucien; Vincenzio Antinori, an astronomer, director of the physics museum in Florence; Paola Savi, Professor of Natural History at Pisa. These were advised by Sir John Bowring, a liberal business man and traveller. These conferences continued annually, changing their place of meeting—like the German conferences—from year to year. The dates and places were as follows: Turin, 1840; Florence, 1841; Padua, 1842; Lucca, 1843; Milan, 1844; Naples, 1845; Genoa, 1846; Venice, 1847. Attendance rose from 421 (in 1839) to 1,778 (in 1847). In 1848 the meetings were suppressed and only three more were held before 1907, when they were revived on a purely scientific basis (as 'Societa Italiana per il progresso della scienze'). As *Revista Europea* said in 1839, describing one of them, these conferences were gatherings 'of illustrious men, of scholars come together from every part of the fair land where "si" is heard, to confer, to become mutually acquainted, to co-operate fraternally, in the splendour and progress of science, in the glory of the common fatherland.'

'The Congresses,' it has been said of these Italian assemblies, 'were at first colourless but very practical gatherings of naturalists and scientists, who met under government patronage; but it was impossible for Italians of different states to come together without giving something of a national complexion to their meetings. Economic questions suggested a customs-league, social problems led up to politics, geography to free-spoken talk of Italy. The

Scientific Congresses were among the forces that made the new nationalism; and the Pope and the Duke of Modena were wise in their generation, when they forbad their subjects to attend them. It was the same school that gave the first serious impulse to railways. . . . It was not only that railways promised to develop trade; the patriots recognised that they would be the most potent of material interests to bind the peninsula together.'[1] It might be noted that at the conferences of German Scientists and Doctors in 1847 a speaker stressed the significance of the fact that the same age in Germany produced both the scientific conferences and also railways. Progress, it was stated in the Italian *Annali* in 1839, 'comes on iron rails,' and at the 1847 congress at Venice it was declared that railways would 'stitch the boot of Italy.'

The resemblance between the German and Italian conferences was due to the fact that similar causes produced similar results. Paradoxically it was in England, where the situation was very different, that the German organisation exercised an immediate and lasting influence.

From about 1826 complaints began to be heard from leading scientists in this country that science was developing more slowly than on the continent. Moreover, the growth of trade and manufacture (in advance of Germany) made scientific advance an urgent necessity. From this point of view the Royal Society was by this time in a highly unsatisfactory condition. It had come into being to harness science to practical tasks, but by the early nineteenth century it was no longer fulfilling this function. Among those who voiced feelings of dissatisfaction were Charles Babbage in his *Reflexions on the Decline of Science in England* (1830). This work was the subject of a review-article published anonymously in the *Quarterly Review*[2] by Sir David Brewster, who was convinced that the problem was one in which England could learn much from foreign countries.

Attention was bound to be paid to Germany, because the conferences of Scientists and Doctors were becoming known

[1] Bolton King, *A History of Italian Unity*, 3rd impression, London, 1924, I, pp. 150–1.
[2] Vol. XLIII, p. 305 seq.

through the small number of British scholars who attended their meetings. Among them was Babbage, who visited the important Berlin congress in 1828. Three years later James F. W. Johnston published an article on the German organisation in the *Edinburgh Journal of Science* in which there is the following description: 'The first object of these meetings is to promote . . . acquaintance and friendly personal intercourse among men of science; but other great and perhaps more important benefits have grown spontaneously out of them. They draw public attention to science and scientific men, and make people inquire concerning both them and their pursuits. They exalt science in general estimation, and with it those who devote themselves to its advancement; and, above all, they spur on the Governments of the different states to examine into and ameliorate the condition of their scientific institutions; and to seek for men of true science to fill the chairs of public instruction. Such and similar benefits have already resulted from the meetings in Germany.' Johnston was exaggerating the consequences of the German conferences, viewing them too much in the light of the particular needs of science in his own country. On the threshold of the English industrial revolution the decay of the Royal Society made it urgently necessary to create something to take its place. The conferences in Germany seemed to offer the possibility of an alternative. 'Might not similar results,' he added, 'in our own country be looked for from a similar institution?'[1] So it was that the German conferences of Scientists and Doctors, having in their origins been at least indirectly influenced by the Royal Society, served as the model for the British Association, the first meeting of which was held at York in 1831. As Howarth says, 'it has to be admitted that the British Association was founded on a German model.'[2]

The resemblances are well illustrated in the speech of Harcourt which[3] led to the actual foundation of the British

---

[1] Quoted by O. J. R. Howarth, *The British Association for the Advancement of Science. A Retrospect, 1831–1921*, London, 1922, p. 7.

[2] *Ibid.*, p. 7.

[3] Quoted in *ibid.*, p. 17 seq.

Association. He pointed out that 'the Royal Society no longer performs the part of promoting natural knowledge by any such exertions as those which we now propose to revive. As a body, it scarcely labours itself, and does not attempt to guide the labours of others.' It happens, he observed, that 'when any science becomes popular, and those who interest themselves in its advancement perceive the necessity of working for it by united exertions, that science is detached from the central body; first one fragment falls off, and then another; colony after colony dissevers itself from the declining empire and by degrees the common-wealth of science is dissolved.' In other words, 'as the facts and speculations in any department of knowledge are multiplied, the study of it has a tendency to engross and confine the views of those by whom it is cultivated.' 'Nothing, I think,' he continued, 'could be a more disastrous event for the sciences than that one of them should be in any manner dissociated from another, and nothing can conduce more to prevent that dissociation than the bringing into mutual contact men who have exercised great and equal powers of mind upon different pursuits,' and he developed this idea in the following passage:

But even the experienced in science will benefit by consulta-tion with each other; for there are different degrees of experi-ence, and no solitary industry or talent can ever hope to equal the power of combined wisdom and concerted labour. Above all, consider, gentlemen, the excitement to exertion which will be felt by those who are solicited to undertake an inquiry at one of these meetings, and pledged to produce the investigations at another. The greatest minds require to be urged by outward impulses, and there is no impulse more powerful than that which is exercised by publicly esteemed bodies of men. Even Newton's papers might have remained unfinished, but for the incentive of such a solicitation. In a letter which I have lately received from Mr. Conybeare . . . the benefit in these respects which may be looked for from a general scientific combination is described with the energy of his ardent and comprehensive genius. 'Your proposal,' he says, 'for ingrafting on the annual reunion of scientific men, a system of effecting such a concentration of the talent of the country as might tend more effectually to consolidate and combine its scattered powers, to direct its investigations to the points which an extensive survey thus generalised would indicate as the most important—benefited by all the aid which the union of powerful minds, the enlarged comparison of different views, and a general system of intellectual co-operation could not fail to afford, fills me with visions too extensive almost to allow me to write with sufficient calmness of approbation. The combined advantages, including at once the most powerful stimulus and the most efficient guidance of scientific research, which might emanate from such a point of central union seem to me to be beyond calculation. If views like those you have sketched could be realised, they would almost give a local habitation and a name to the philosophical academy of Bacon's Atlantis, when "divers meetings and consults" of the united body of Depradators, Compilers, Pioneers, etc., suggested new experiments of a higher light and more penetrating nature to the lamps, and these a₁ length yielded materials to the interpreters of nature.'

This led him to the practical suggestion that 'members shall meet for one week in every year at different places in rotation; in order by these migratory visits to extend the sphere of the Association, to meet the convenience of distant districts in turn and to animate the spirit of phil-osophy in all the places through which the meetings may move, without rendering them burthensome to any.'

The German conferences reflect the trend towards the integration of knowledge among bourgeois intellectuals in the light of the changing needs of their class in the decades preceding its bid for political power. In the German organisation this aspect was often expressed indirectly and tentatively in a manner corresponding to the relatively backward economic and social conditions in Germany at the time. In England the bourgeoisie was more advanced, and its desire to bring all aspects of knowledge into relation-ship with each other manifested itself more confidently and with wider vision.

Nevertheless the conferences of Scientists and Doctors, as compared with the other academic and scientific conferences of the period, show the bourgeois movement in Germany in its most positive light, least corrupted by the contradictions which already before 1848 were—as will be shown—to force its social and ideological programme into a pattern which can be recognised as a pre-natal stage of German imperialism. The reason why these particular conferences can be thus described is connected with the fundamental fact that the development—through science—of the forces of production is a progressive feature of any social or political order. The Scientists and Doctors were the first nationally organised body of German intellectuals at the beginning (in Germany) of the age of modern industry, which, as Marx stated, 'makes science a productive force distinct from labour and presses it into the service of capital.'[1]

However, Germany's social and economic backwardness had the result in these conferences that only rarely do we find a bold expression of faith in the power of science to change society. An example can be quoted from the meeting in 1839. Obscurantism, a speaker declared, was seeking to rob science of its victories. The fruits of science, he said, 'are the final results of the efforts of past centuries and certainly no future age will allow itself to be robbed of them, no matter how much cunning obscurantists, groping around in the dark and denouncing us as atheists, endeavour to destroy those precious fruits and to bring back the times of the barbarous Middle Ages.'[2] 'We owe the great progress,' he continued, 'which chemistry, natural science, anatomy and physiology have made, pre-eminently to the efforts of gifted and talented doctors who were convinced that medicine had to be given a scientific basis, not through metaphysical speculation, but that this aim could be attained only by the broadening and enriching of the physical sciences and by their successful application to medicine. The efforts of those doctors of the present time, who are familiar with the history of medicine and its fortunes, are therefore not directed to the carrying out of systems but rather to the exact observation of nature and the appearance and course of disease. They are concerned to work out the factors that cause it, to investigate effects of any remedies that are tried, to formulate the results of their observations in principles derived from experience and to interpret them in terms of principles of physiology.'[3] But this tribute to the revolutionary power of experimental science led the

---

[1] *Capital*, Allen and Unwin ed., p. 355.

[2] *Amtlicher Bericht*, 1839, pp. 14–15.   [3] *Ibid.*, pp. 27–8.

same speaker to an idealist conclusion which in its context was consistent with acceptance of the existing order of things. 'Each step,' he said, 'which the investigator takes in the field of natural science compels him to admire the inner harmony of the world-order and brings him nearer to the recognition of the divine spirit which ever rules in nature and which compels him to revere and worship it and summons him to act according to the laws of reason and morality.'[1] It is significant that the same speaker, after saying that economic developments and the growth of science had changed the character of German society, declared that, liberated from feudal restraints, men could now enjoy a higher level of well-being and cultural achievement under the protection of the princes. It is also worth noting that in 1842 the attempt was made—without success, as it happened—to add a clause in the statutes to the effect that 'a greater field of activity for the society' could be attained 'by co-operation with the German governments, especially the German Confederation.' One does not need a deep knowledge of German history to realise how illusory was the emancipation of which this member boasted nor much political insight to guess the price that would have had to be paid in terms of liberal principles for the collaboration involved in the latter proposal.

We are justified in attaching importance to these aspects in the discussions of the Scientists and Doctors since by implication at least they suggest a problem which will force itself on our attention in the conferences to be examined in the next chapter. Though the Scientists and Doctors affirmed the importance of science, they did so with moderation and caution. The conferences of Classical Philologists rested on the frank declaration of the value of idealism as a stabilising factor in an age disturbed by the rise of a proletariat class. It was, in fact, in the most obviously 'cultural' aspects that the German intellectuals were most deeply sensitive to the threatened values.

[1] *Ibid.*, p. 31.

CHAPTER II

THE CONFERENCES OF CLASSICAL PHILOLOGISTS, SECONDARY
SCHOOLMASTERS AND ORIENTALISTS

The Berlin conference of Scientists and Doctors in 1828
was a noteworthy occasion in the history of the intellectual
middle class. Germany had never before witnessed so
important a gathering of intellectuals so widely representative of the country as a whole. This fact deserves greater
attention than it has received, and the same applies to the
centenary celebrations of Göttingen University in 1837.
Though not as important as the Berlin gathering, this had
a comparable significance in bringing intellectuals together
and providing—by chance rather than by design—an
occasion for the discussion of problems of common interest.
Moreover, the Göttingen celebrations occurred at a crucial
point—on the eve of the dismissal of the seven professors for
their action in protesting against the autocratic and uncon-
stitutional behaviour of King Ernst August who, on coming
to the throne of Hannover, declared the relatively liberal
constitution of 1833 invalid. This crisis helped to stimulate
the political consciousness of many members of the middle
class, especially intellectuals, and to give them an added
sense of comradeship under the impact of a political attack
indirectly affecting them all. 'The constitutional breach
in Hannover . . .,' it has been well said, 'influenced wide
sections of German scholars in the direction of liberalism. . . .
Under the impression of this event the professors of the
German universities drew closer to each other and in the
fate of the Seven saw themselves all threatened and hit.'[1]

It was from discussions among scholars assembled at
Göttingen for the centenary festivities that the plan emerged
for the conferences which are to be analysed in the following
pages. In his memoirs Friedrich Kohlrausch, an educational
administrator in Hannover, describes the circumstances:

[1] Adolf Stoll. *Friedrich Karl von Savigny, Professorenjahre in Berlin
1810–1842*, Berlin, 1929, p. 381.

'From the meeting of many university teachers and school-masters . . . there also emerged the idea of regular gatherings of philologists and schoolmasters successively in different parts of Germany. Unless I am mistaken, it was Thiersch who instigated it and immediately collected opinions and signatures in favour of the plan which was rapidly drawn up. I was one of the first to sign under the statutes of 20th September, 1837, and in this sense can claim the honour of being one of the founders of these important conferences.'[1] At the sixth conference the Vice-President was careful to remind members of their indebtedness to the informal discussions at Göttingen: 'We are particularly pleased that so many of those worthy men are with us to-day who for the first time six years ago, at the centenary festival of the Georgia-Augusta University, had the idea of creating our Society and whom we quite correctly regard as the actual founders.'[2] Apart from Thiersch and Kohlrausch, those who signed the statutes included Jakob and Wilhelm Grimm, and Ewald (three of the 'Göttingen Seven'), Ritschl (professor at Breslau, chiefly known for his work on Plautus), Ferdinand Ranke (brother of the famous historian, headmaster of the grammar school in Göttingen, later of the Friedrich-Wilhelms-Gymnasium in Berlin) and other university teachers and schoolmasters from Halle, Brunswick, Hannover, Jena, etc. In addition there was a Dr. Rost who after Thiersch played the biggest single part in establishing the Society. Alexander von Humboldt, conspicuous in some of the conferences of Scientists and Doctors, was not on the list, but the proceedings of the second conference contain a note to the effect that the organisation was regarded as having come into being under his auspices. The first conference was held at Nuremberg in 1838, despite the misgivings of the Bavarian Minister of the Interior, who made Thiersch personally responsible for keeping the discussions away from politics.

[1] *Erinnerungen aus meinem Leben*, Hannover, 1863, p. 381.

[2] *Verhandlungen der sechsten Versammlung deutscher Philologen und Schulmänner in Cassel, 1843*, p. 12. As in the case of the Scientists and Doctors the proceedings were usually published the following year at the place of meeting. It will be noted that the Classical Philologists, too, were careful to describe themselves as 'German.'

Thiersch, whose role in these conferences corresponded
to that of Oken in those of the Scientists and Doctors, was
a prominent figure in German liberalism in this period.
His contribution to German education has earned respect
for its liberal purpose.   This is reflected in his exchange of
views with a minister of the Bavarian government.   The
latter had declared: 'The state needs the largest number of
its servants for restricted activity. . . . It is for this that
they should be prepared and guided.   If men of greater
distinction come along they are useless.   It is therefore
reasonable to lower the demands made on the schools and
to limit the character of the instruction.'[1]   To this narrowly
utilitarian and reactionary formulation Thiersch opposed
a broader and deeper conception, stressing the formative
value of classical education and its value as a basis for the
study of law and theology.   The grammar schools, he said,
should not overload their syllabus with a mass of extraneous
and disconnected subjects but should concentrate on the
need to provide a sound training in philosophy.   He fought
against the tendency in Bavaria to degrade the function of
universities and to limit their freedom.   The University
of Landshut, for example, had been suffering under the
restrictive legislation imposed by Montgelas, a minister of
the Bavarian government, who had enforced periodical
examinations and a prescribed course of study.   After it
became known that the king proposed to have it transferred
to Munich, Thiersch argued that the new university should
have a full measure of academic freedom, believing this to
be necessary for the proper development of the students'
character.   He pointed out that, though in England the
free activity of students in universities was restricted, this
was more than made good by the liberty of the national life
as a whole.[2]   The king studied his opinions on the subject
with the result that the University of Munich was granted
the freedom advocated by Thiersch.   The same anxiety
about academic freedom led him in 1837 to publish a
pamphlet *On the New Attacks on German Universities.*

[1] Quoted by Thiersch, *Über gelehrte Schulen*, I, p. 16.

[2] Thiersch dealt with these aspects in *ibid.*, II, the section entitled 'Die
hohen Schulen, mit besonderer Rücksicht auf die Universität München.'

This was in part an answer to Diesterweg's pamphlet of the previous year *On the Decay of German Universities*, in which he demanded tighter supervision and discipline to counteract the alleged moral decay in the universities.

Thiersch's activities in the years immediately before the proposal to create an annual conference of Classical Philologists—we shall refer to them in this abbreviated form— had included a visit to the meetings of the Scientists and Doctors, where he read a paper in 1835—an example of the frequent personal links between the different conferences. The example of the Scientists and Doctors was in fact extremely influential in suggesting the idea of these conferences. When the question of revising the statutes was discussed in 1843 it was stated that the scientific conferences had been kept in mind from the start. However, between the two series of conferences there was the important difference that those of the Classical Philologists included secondary schoolmasters in addition to university teachers. In this respect they were unique among all the academic conferences of the time and for this reason a few words should be said regarding the position of secondary schoolmasters in the German middle class at this time.

Throughout the first half of the nineteenth century elementary teachers were, generally speaking, subordinated to the church; this was as anxious as the state that they should not develop such independence of outlook as might make them dissatisfied with their humble station. The situation was very different in the case of secondary schoolmasters. The reason lay partly in the fact that as early as 1787 a Secondary School Board had been created in Prussia by von Zedlitz and placed under the Ministry of Finance. That is to say, by the end of the eighteenth century secondary education had been taken out of the hands of the church and put under the supervision of secular authority. Secondary schoolmasters, moreover, were mostly products of the universities. This not only gave them a higher prestige but it also meant that they inherited the tradition of freedom which the universities embodied even in the age of absolutism. Whereas throughout the first part of the nineteenth century elementary teachers were usually ranked among the lower

classes, secondary schoolmasters were socially more or less
in the same general category as university teachers. Certainly, a distinguished classical master at a grammar school
or, as in the case of Hegel, the headmaster of a large and
important school were regarded by the public as approximately equal in status to a university professor. The
combination therefore of secondary schoolmasters and
university teachers was not an unnatural one, and it reflected
moreover the growing habit of collaboration within an
increasingly coherent middle class.[1]

The precise position of secondary schoolmasters in the
conferences was defined in section 4 of the statutes, which
stated: 'Every classical philologist can become a member
of the Society provided he can furnish evidence to the state
to which he belongs that he teaches or has taught at a
grammar school or university or that he holds an official
post. Also schoolmasters who are concerned with the
other branches of higher public instruction, such as mathematics, physics, history and geography, are invited to take
part in the gatherings. In that case they will represent
only the subjects that they teach.' Thus, a distinction, and
an important one, was made between those who teach the
classics and those occupied with other subjects. The
former were to have full rights of active membership, while
the latter were only to be present, as it were, by invitation
and were to speak only in the name of their particular field
of study.

The same part of the statutes contains this statement:
'The members of the Society of Schoolmasters of North
Germany (*Verein nordischer Schulmänner*) are invited also
to take part in this organisation.' This was a reference to
a body founded in Lübeck in 1834. At the first meeting
of the Classical Philologists members were notified of a
letter from a grammar school headmaster in Lübeck,
offering the full collaboration of this organisation. The
problem proved to be more difficult than expected and
another appeal was made at the conference in 1840.

[1] For a short analysis of the social position of the German schoolmaster
cf. R. H. Samuel and R. Hinton Thomas, *Education and Society in Modern
Germany*, London, 1949, p. 55 seq.

Returning to his original proposal he wrote a further letter containing this significant passage: 'This (i.e. the combined organisation) could help to put an end to unpleasant cliquish activity and become, like a spiritual Customs Union, a splendid bond uniting the whole country.'[1]

The relations within the Society were not free from difficulties, mainly owing to disagreements among the schoolmasters. A split occurred when in 1846 a group of teachers from 'Realschulen' (secondary schools offering a shorter and more utilitarian course than the grammar schools) seceded. One speaker explained the position thus: 'The "Realschule" teachers formed part of the Philologists' Society until the Cassel meeting (i.e. 1843). Since then they have held separate meetings for their particular group in different towns and the Classical Philologists were not included in the invitations. They have thus detached themselves from the general conference; to use a favourite expression, they have emancipated themselves like a colony from its metropolis.' The nature of the split was significant. Trade and manufacture were developing sufficiently to make it less easy for the representatives of the more practical 'Realschulen' to work in easy partnership with those who asserted the supremacy of education based on the classics. In due course, however, steps were considered, not to reunite the 'Realschule' teachers with the Classical Philologists, but to absorb them into a broader teachers' organisation. In 1847 Rost was able to announce to the conference that the attempt to maintain a separate association of 'Realschule' teachers was coming to an end. 'On this very day,' he reported, 'the "Realschule" teachers' society is holding its last meeting and in all probability it will then cease to exist in accordance with the decision that a general teachers' society should be established to include both humanists and "realists." About the details of this reunion nothing can at this stage be published nor can the matter be here discussed.'[2] There is no need to follow this development further, except to notice that in the flood of the bourgeois-revolutionary movement in 1848 a General

[1] The letter is printed in full in the *Verhandlungen*, 1840.
[2] *Ibid.*, 1847, p. 74.

German Teachers' Society was formed. But the struggle between the two groups of secondary schoolmasters was not settled by this measure, and later in the century it was continued in the rivalry between the Society of Grammar School Teachers and the Society of 'Realschule' Teachers.

Turning to the Orientalists, the first step was taken in September, 1843, when a chance meeting of two professors from Halle, two from Leipzig and a government official from Altenburg led to a proposal that German Orientalists should confer annually and invite their colleagues from abroad. This suggestion was at once accepted by those present who with two additions immediately formed themselves into a provisional committee. As a first step the intention was to summon a large gathering of Orientalists to Leipzig. But at a subsequent meeting of the committee in March, 1844, it was agreed that instead they should try to join the conference of Classical Philologists due to take place that year in Dresden. The suggestion was cordially accepted by the Philologists and the government authorities in Saxony sanctioned the increase in numbers involved. In July, 1844, came the formal invitation from the President. One of the Classical Philologists expressed the fear that the change might undermine the homogeneous character of their organisation, but Thiersch pointed out that the statutes allowed for the expansion of the activities to cover language study as a whole.

It was agreed that, in order to make possible the maximum amount of common activity, the Classical Philologists— following the procedure of the Scientists and Doctors— should hold all meetings likely to be of general interest at the beginning and the Orientalists at the end. The Orientalists were thus absorbed into the larger body which changed its title accordingly. The Orientalists held their special sessions in a room set aside for them, their members were marked with an asterisk in the list of those present and their minutes did not form part of the main official report. Thus the following note was added to the statutes: 'Since the 7th (Dresden) conference the German Orientalists have also joined the Society as a special section.'

These details are significant for reasons best summed up

in this statement: 'The Classical Philologist, in the previous century the very embodiment of the rank-conscious scholar in the stereotyped sense, brought one survival of his cliquish habits into the gathering of his colleagues, for he described it as the congress of "Classical Philologists and Orientalists." This "and" is the last sign of the closed guild of the "classical" philologist who would like to regard the man from the unclassical sphere of oriental language study merely as a back-bencher.'[1]

The admission of the Orientalists on these terms raised the question whether, in general, the creation of specialist sections should be permitted. In 1845 the acting President pointed out that in the previous year the conference had rejected this on principle, though it had admitted the Orientalists.[2] The matter was clarified in 1846 when the President said: 'Similarly the question whether sections can be formed is to be regarded as settled. By sections, however, we understand not haphazard gatherings . . . but definite branches of knowledge.'[3]

The Scientists and Doctors had also given serious attention to this problem, which was important for the Classical Philologists for the same reason in view of the wider aims of their organisation.

These were summarised in the presidential address in 1844. 'Let us confess at the outset,' it was stated, 'that the personal relationships between many of us are not what they should and could be. Some live in isolation as a result of their social and official position and usually have no direct intercourse with other specialists in their field. Such intercourse protects us from one-sidedness, fills in gaps in our knowledge and ability and is always valuable as a stimulus. Others rob themselves of this advantage and separate themselves from the bonds which should unite all citizens of the republic of learning and particularly those working in the same province. . . . (Our conferences) are intended to awaken, increase and maintain the consciousness of spiritual unity and the centripetal power of scholarship.

---

[1] Riehl, *op. cit.*, pp. 233–4. [2] *Verhandlungen*, 1845, p. 6 seq.
[3] *Ibid.*, 1846, p. 16.

They are to provide a meeting-point for all, in which they learn to feel themselves as unifying parts of the whole and in their turn, from the living force of the total body, derive stimulus for joyful activity in their special fields.'[1] The aim, he said, was 'the creation, restoration and consolidation of friendly personal relations and of a humane *esprit de corps* amongst us.'[2] This was the ideal which had inspired Thiersch from the very beginning. 'The supreme aim,' he wrote to Gottfried Hermann in 1837, 'is to bring together the different branches and schools in the greatest numbers. With this we link the hope that discussion and personal intercourse will resolve antagonisms and will foster many things that can best be advanced by collaboration, provided that we fix our attention on what is sound and brush aside all endeavours that are powerless or confused.'[3] In the statutes it was laid down that one of the tasks of the organisation was 'to remove scholarship from the conflict of the various schools and, allowing for differences of views and tendencies, in the essential matters to maintain the agreement and mutual respect of those working on the same task with seriousness of purpose and ability.'

Bearing in mind the cliquish squabbles that had so often marred the relations of German scholars, even of those concerned with the same branch of study, it must be said that the atmosphere of these gatherings was on the whole remarkably amicable. Friction was not totally lacking. For example, there was one occasion when less careful handling might have led to serious consequences. This happened at Dresden in 1844. A headmaster from Bremen delivered what was intended to be a humorous lecture on the stature of Horace 'with special reference to the culinary art of the Ancients and an excursus on the treatment of crab by the Romans.' The President (Thiersch) intervened, fearing the susceptibility of members, and persuaded the speaker not to finish his address, but not before disparaging remarks had been made about diplomats and Jews. This was all the more painful since Prince John

---

[1] *Ibid.*, 1844, pp. 5–6.   [2] *Ibid.*, 1844, p. 5.

[3] The whole letter is quoted by H. J. W. Thiersch, *Friedrich Thiersch's Leben*, Leipzig and Heidelberg, 1866, II, pp. 466–8.

of Saxony was in the audience. Thiersch rose to say that
nothing must be said to hurt anyone's feelings and spoke
strongly against the views expressed. On the following
day the speaker wrote to the President to say that it had not
been his intention to insult anybody or any section of the
community. But this did not close the episode. Bergk
published (in the *Journal of Classical Scholarship*) a personal
attack on Thiersch whom he accused of highhanded
behaviour on this occasion and in the conferences in general.
Thiersch took the matter very much to heart. He could
not attend the meeting in the following year, but he chose
to absent himself from the gathering in 1846 and 1847.
There was a parallel in the conferences of Scientists and
Doctors where disharmony crept in between Oken and
others, with the result that Oken stayed away from a
number of meetings, though he remained in the background
as councillor and friend.

In the main, however, the spirit of co-operation was so
striking that some, who attended their first meeting with
a cynical predisposition to criticise, were forced to revise
their judgment. Ritschl is a case in point. The first
occasion he was present was at Mannheim in 1839. He
reported mockingly that he found there 'a massive core
of German philologists . . . well covered in a Baden
nutshell.'[1] He was repelled by 'the dry scholarship and
boring character'[2] of the meeting and was only too glad
to escape back to Bonn. The following year in Gotha,
however, he began to see the activities in a more favourable
light. Before he participated, he wrote in 1840, he always
regarded these 'philological autumn manoeuvres' with
supercilious amusement, 'but to my shame I must say
that I came away with warm interest for this institution.
From the personal point of view there are very pleasant
people in this mob of philologists,[3] and more intellectual

---

[1] The reference is to the predominance of members from Baden.
Ritschl's picturesque (and mildly cynical) phrase reads in German:
'Kernmasse deutscher Philologie . . . eingehüllt in reichliche Badensische
Nussschalen.'

[2] Quoted by Otto Ribbeck, *Friedrich Wilhelm Ritschl*, Leipzig, 1879–81,
II, p. 43.

[3] 'Philologenvolk'—the phrase denotes a measure of contempt.

stimulus emerges than I had previously thought. The feeling of general harmony, which in fact inspired everyone, was very beneficial.'[1]

This was one of the main objectives of the founders who thought that, important though they were, papers and scholarly discussions should not be an end in themselves. We need not therefore bother ourselves much with the technical aspects. The subjects ranged from specialised themes of the narrowest philological interest to speeches of more general appeal, such as Welcker's talk on 'The Significance of Philology,'[2] which was read (in Welcker's absence in Greece) by Ritschl at Bonn. At the same meeting a message was prepared in honour of A. W. Schlegel, the senior member present, and a special coin was ordered to be struck in memory of Otfried Müller, the celebrated Göttingen philologist who had died the previous year in Athens. In Cassel Spohr conducted a performance of Mendelssohn's setting of the choruses from Sophocles' *Antigone*. In Dresden a solemn presentation was made to Gottfried Hermann, professor in Leipzig, well-known for his work on metre and Greek grammar, who had accepted the responsibilities of the post of President despite old age and infirmity. Occasionally something of practical importance emerged. For example, there was the decision (at Bonn) to found a Society of Friends of Antiquity in the Rhineland; the suggestion came from a member who had just returned from Rome where he was impressed by the flourishing Institute of Archæology.

The social pursuits were varied and sometimes ambitious. There was, for example, the special dinner at Königswinter (near Bonn), where the assembly was honoured by the king of Prussia. On this occasion, as on others, members derived an obvious delight from the presence of royalty. Kohlrausch, for instance, records his joy at sitting next to the Duke at the luncheon given by him in honour of those attending the Gotha conference. 'The reigning Duke of Coburg-Gotha,' he wrote, 'father of the present Duke and of Prince Albert—recently married to Queen Victoria—paid

[1] Quoted by Ribbeck, *op. cit.*, II, p. 44.
[2] Reprinted in his *Kleine Schriften*, IV, p. 1 *seq.*

us the special attention of inviting the whole conference to lunch at Reinhardsbrunn. The company was so large that it had to be held in the open air. But it was a lovely October day and the Duke, with respect for bookish scholars partly spoilt by the seclusion of their studies, had the kind thought of wearing his hat and invited the whole company to do likewise. I sat next to the Duke, and Thiersch sat on his other side. Opposite us sat the present Duke, a young and lively gentleman of twenty-one. I found it very interesting to make the acquaintance here of part of the Coburg family, one of whom had ascended the Belgian throne and two of whom stood so near to the thrones of England and Portugal. The Duke, a handsome man with expressive and attractive features and the most perfect manners of a prince who is conscious of his position but is able to respect the virtues of others, discoursed in the most informal way with his neighbours at table, not about the usual subjects of court conversation, but about those which concerned our meeting in Gotha.'[1] Kohlrausch's description of other aspects of the Gotha conference is worth quoting: 'The conference of university teachers and schoolmasters in Gotha lived up to the expectations which one was justified in entertaining for such a gathering. It was less the prepared lectures on scholarly matters (which indeed are mainly of a kind better read than heard) that claimed our attention than the exchange of ideas and experiences . . . and above all the personal intercourse outside the public sessions between old and new acquaintances, even between opponents who had not known each other before and unexpectedly form quite a different opinion of one another when they see each other face to face. The tone in the learned journals had become, in fact, unnecessarily sharp and bitter and it was the humanists who frequently were the least humane. The solitary study does not soften indignation, when it has been aroused, and even the lecturer's desk does not encourage moderation, for the speaker hears only himself. But when two men have once spoken together in good company and drunk a

[1] *Op. cit.*, pp. 342–3.

glass of wine together . . . they can never again be spiteful about each other in their writings.'[1]

As in the case of the other conferences the idea of building friendly relations between scholars has to be seen in connection with the broader purpose of making the gatherings focal points of 'national' activity. Thiersch's conception of the conferences of Classical Philologists was similar to Oken's of those of the Scientists and Doctors. They were, as he said, to embrace all Germany.

It is true that many of the addresses were far too academic and remote to have any relationship to anything outside themselves. Even when a member spoke, at the Nuremberg meeting, about the teaching of history 'national' arguments were conspicuous by their absence, though the theme lent itself to treatment from this point of view. Outlining a plan for a history textbook, he said: 'Since the textbook is not concerned with the history of nations but with the history of the human race, single elements from national history . . . have only to be included in so far as they are important.'[2] Such a view was more characteristic of the cosmopolitanism of the eighteenth century than of the main ideological currents in the age of the nation-state. Nevertheless, the national character of the conferences was repeatedly emphasised.

The statement of the President at Cassel in 1846 can serve as an example. 'It is true,' he declared, 'that we are sorry to miss many who up till now have taken the most lively interest in the affairs of our Society, but are kept away by unexpected hindrances.[3] But all the true German states, Swabia, Bavaria, Thuringia, Saxony, Hannover, Westphalia, Holstein, have sent their representatives. Moreover, we regard it as a specially favourable sign that we see in our midst several guests from beyond the Elbe, who previously were accustomed to meet in a small society following similar aims but more local in character.'[4] In the same spirit the statutes recommended that the conferences should instigate 'large-scale philological enterprises

[1] *Ibid.*, pp. 340–1.   [2] *Verhandlungen*, 1838, p. 46.
[3] Clearly a reference, amongst others, to Thiersch. Cf. p. 60.
[4] *Ibid.*, 1843, p. 12.

which require the united effort of a greater number of people.'
This was an idea common to all the conferences of the time,
as was seen with regard to the Scientists and Doctors and
as will be shown in connection with the 'Germanisten.'
As far as this particular proposal is concerned, little was
actually achieved, though one important concrete suggestion
was put forward.   This was made in 1843 by a member who
thought that the time had come to prepare, with the collaboration of teachers in the areas involved, a map covering
'the whole area of the German language' and showing all
the different dialects,[1] a task which was more properly
that of the 'Germanisten.'

The need to bring people together in order that they might
reach a common understanding about the main problems
was sometimes, it is true, formulated in European rather
than merely German terms, as by Thiersch himself in 1839.
After saying that, in an age of increasing communication
and trade, men required more than ever a common basis,
he argued that classical studies formed 'a generally known
and unspoilt currency, recognised by all, for the spiritual
exchange of European culture.'[2]   But one is struck rather
by the number of occasions on which the stress shifts
from the European to the national aspect of the Society,
as in a speech of Thiersch in 1840 dealing with the organisation of education.   In the previous year the conference had
voted against a proposal for a unified system of education
throughout the whole country.   Thiersch explained that
he thought the decision was correct and the reasons are
significant.   'The impossibility of such a plan,' he said,
'should not be derived from the regional differences within
the German nation, from the divergent stages of culture and
intellectual needs of individuals and not from their confessional differentiation.   The differences among the German
states . . . do not affect the roots.   Also, apart from
certain theological disciplines, Germany has not got a
Catholic or Protestant type of scholarship, but a German
type, and the genius of our fatherland will protect us in the
future from such a cleavage.'[3]   His objections to the

[1] *Ibid.*, 1843, pp. 37–40.   [2] *Ibid.*, 1839, p. 9.
[3] *Ibid.*, 1840, p. 18.

proposal put forward the previous year did not arise from
any doubts on this score, but rather from the knowledge
that the establishment of a unified school system for the
nation as a whole presupposed a settled and agreed basis
on which to work and at the moment this was lacking.   To
create it was the purpose of these and similar conferences.
Again, in 1850 the President, after saying that the meetings
of 1848 and 1849 had had to be cancelled owing to political
events 'in our common German fatherland,' lamented—
with reference to the outcome of 1848—that many of the
hopes cherished at previous meetings had not been realised.
'It is not without sorrow,' he said, 'that I must say that in
the present year the conditions in Germany have by no
means taken the course which, as far as my feelings and
understanding are concerned, could not but be desired by
a gathering of German scholars; for such a conference has
its roots essentially in consciousness of the unity of the
spirit in the German nation, in German scholarship and
learning . . . for in German scholarship the spiritual bond
and the inner unity of the people has long existed and every
separatist tendency has long been abandoned.   For it was
in German scholarship that the German spirit has had to
seek refuge, it has had to withdraw into this certain and
invulnerable place of refuge and hide there at a time when
external forces had sworn to destroy it.'[1]

Just as the Scientists and Doctors, conscious of their
importance as guardians and sponsors of the national idea,
missed no opportunity of establishing contact with other
groups of intellectuals in the course of their peregrinations
through Germany, the same is true of the Classical Philologists, though there does not seem to have been the same
enthusiasm on the part of other bodies to associate themselves with the conferences of Classical Philologists.   The
most noteworthy contact was with the conference of German
Philosophers in 1847, with whom the Scientists and Doctors
also established relations.   The minutes of the Gotha
meeting of the Classical Philologists contain a summary of
a speech by Rost, in which he pointed out that a few days
before a 'Society of German Philosophers' had met, likewise

[1] *Ibid.*, 1850, p. 15.

in Gotha. All members had asked him, he said, to convey the fraternal greetings of the Philosophers 'and to report their conviction that philosophy was valueless without philology and on the basis of this conviction to express their desire that occasionally the Classical Philologists should pay them a visit—in future they would meet shortly before the conferences of the Classical Philologists.'[1]

This reference demands a brief digression about the activity of the Philosophers. On 7th June, 1847, Immanuel Hermann Fichte, professor at Tübingen from 1842[2]—son of the more famous author of the *Addresses to the German Nation*—wrote to the Duke of Coburg-Gotha: 'It has for a long time been my own wish and that of several like-minded men to organise a conference of the best known German philosophers this autumn in some suitable place. The choice of a satisfactory place for this meeting however aroused many misgivings and doubts. Then I had the happy idea of placing the first conference of German philosophers under the auspices of Your Royal Highness, at the same time of requesting you, Sir, to grant us permission to meet in the town of Gotha. Your Royal Highness, expert in this field of study, will certainly be convinced about the importance at the present time of recurrent philosophical conferences and will be willing to take the first of them under his protection.' The Duke, a former student of the younger Fichte, readily consented. Fichte envisaged an annual series of conferences, on the pattern of those of other German scholars, but this plan did not materialise, and no minutes even of this single meeting appear to have been published.[3]

It was not by chance that among German intellectuals in the main fields of learning the philosophers were the

[1] *Ibid.*, 1847, p. 74.

[2] Among his better known works were *Grundzüge zum System der Philosophie*, 1833–46, and *System der Ethik*, 1850–3. Ranke described him as 'obsessed with the idea of becoming the man who would complete the development of speculative philosophy' (*Das Briefwerk*, Hamburg, 1949, p. 273).

[3] The archives of the town of Gotha contain apparently only two documents relating to this conference, Fichte's letter to the Duke (Ernst II, brother of Queen Victoria's Prince Albert) and the reply, signed by a Freiherr von Stein (not to be confused with his famous namesake).

only ones who failed to maintain a flourishing organisation of this type. As has been pointed out, the great struggles of the time were to a considerable extent fought out in the realm of philosophy. In no other sphere, therefore, were the ideological antagonisms so marked, the unifying factors less profound. 'The least successful,' comments Riehl on this interesting situation, 'were the philosophers. They could not advance beyond the narrow academic limits and establish a wider union. The social interest was lacking; at best there was the prospect of a learned tournament, as formerly among the scholastics. Thus it happened that German philosophers of all colours regularly appeared at the conferences of the Scientists or the "Germanisten" or the Philologists, but could not create conferences of their own.'[1]

Many of the main features of these conferences will by now be clear. Some of them can be illustrated by a piece of high-falutin' jingle read to the assembled company during lunch at Jena in 1846, which might be translated thus:

'May Germany grow and prosper through the power of the spirit. O sacred fatherland, glow and shine brightly through the splendour of youth. The strong limbs of the body are still bound beneath the heavy spell of incantations and lullabies, invented by the cunning of the enemy. Germany, they sing, is only good for brooding and for writing poetry; if action is needed, she bravely brings herself to renounce it. O pupil of Hellas, unmask their lies! At the breast of the early world drink the divine joy of creation. Life is only real and true when spirit unites with deeds, when beauty weaves them both together, and when manliness is purified by piety. So, German brethren, be united for the old and just cause. Let everyone study, create—and struggle till the day of victory appears. Thus be it!—sacred spirits, large as life, arise from the grave of the sacred past and be pleased to accept our proffered gift.'

> Deutschland wachse, Deutschland blühe,
> Deutschland blüh durch Geistesmacht,
> Heiliges Vaterland erglühe,
> Leuchte hell durch Jugendpracht.

[1] *Op. cit.*, pp. 243–4.

Deines Leibes kräft'ge Glieder
Immer noch mit schwerem Bann
Fesseln Sprüche, Schlummerlieder,
Die des Feindes Witz ersann.

Nur zum Grübeln, nur zum Dichten,
Tönt ihr Sang, ist Deutschland gut;
Gilt es Handeln—zu verzichten,
Fasst es sich mit frommem Muth.

Hellas' Zögling, straf sie Lügen:
An der Vorwelt Mutterbrust
Trinke du in vollen Zügen
Jedes Schaffens Götterlust.

Nur wenn Geist und That sich einet,
Schönheit beide hold verwebt—
Mannheit sich durch Frommheit reinet,
Dann erst heisst es recht gelebt.—

So für's Alte, so für's Rechte
Deutsche Brüder, seid geeint:
Jeder forsche, bilde—fechte,
Bis der Siegestag erscheint.

Also, sei's!—dem Grabenschoosse
Heil'ger Vorzeit nun entsteigt,
Hohe Geister, menschlich grosse,
Nehmt die Spende frohgeneigt!—

The idea prominent in this poem, that the time had come for German scholarship to devote itself less to theory and more to action, was a conspicuous feature of the time, and we shall discuss it in the course of our analysis of the 'Germanisten.' If this notion receives a greater emphasis on this occasion than in most of the discussions of the Classical Philologists, it was due to the fact that this verse originated under the immediate impression of the crisis in Schleswig-Holstein (which, as will be seen, left its mark so clearly on the 'Germanisten' conferences). The author of this poem felt that Germany had a mission to fulfil, but it is in the name of the past, as the source of truth and justice, that he summons his hearers to unite:

> So für's Alte, so für's Rechte,
> Deutsche Brüder, seid geeint

and it is 'from the grave of the sacred past' that the spirits are conjured up to receive the homage of this gathering of intellectuals:

> dem Grabenschoosse
> Heil'ger Vorzeit nun entsteigt,
> Hohe Geister, menschlich grosse,
> Nehmt die Spende frohgeneigt!

Indeed, one of the striking things about the conferences of the Classical Philologists, as contrasted with those of the Scientists and Doctors and of the 'Germanisten,' is the fact that only rarely do we find in the discussions a markedly forward-looking attitude. In this respect Friedrich Gottlieb Welcker was rather an exception when at Bonn in 1841 he went out of his way to stress the need to guard the fortress of rationalism against the threat of a revival of obscurantism. 'But if the time should ever come,' he declared, 'when hierarchical and mystical interests threatened to impose their limitations on us again, it will be a good fortune if a virile philology upholds in some circles the honour of all that is beautiful and fresh in human life, interprets the miracles of unhindered genius, points to . . . civil liberty and the respect for law which emerge with such definite features from the ancient world, and, when theology tries too much to confiscate the human spirit for future service in heaven, seeks to educate it for joyful activity here on earth.'[1] Generally speaking, however, we find little desire among these learned gentlemen to adjust their conception of humanism to the forward-looking requirements of their own age and circumstances. Few, like Welcker, argued that one of the main tasks of the classical humanist was to develop man's rational understanding of the world in which he lived.

On the contrary, rationalism with its radical implications at this time was a concept that aroused the greatest suspicion among some of the leading spirits in the organisation. An incident occurred at the inaugural conference in 1838 which was by no means as insignificant as might at first appear. A speaker, lecturing on the teaching of religion, let fall in an unguarded moment the remark that 'we philologists are born rationalists.' His

[1] *Verhandlungen*, 1841, p. 46.

F

words caused embarrassment and it was left to Thiersch
to turn the discussion into safer channels by qualifying the
offending statement with the comment: 'yes, all philologists
are born rationalists, but in the good sense like Reuchlin
and Melanchthon.'[1] The debate was then dropped.
During an informal discussion one evening in the course of
the same conference Thiersch, mindful of his undertaking
to prevent the debates from becoming political, grew so
alarmed during a heated argument that he cut it short by
putting the light out.

The most important speech in this connection was certainly
that of Friedrich Jacobs in 1840. By this time Jacobs,
a schoolmaster known mainly for his editions of the classics
and from 1831 curator of the art collections in Gotha, was
so aged and infirm that special arrangements had to be made
to transport him to the conference. His subject was 'The
Ethical Content of Classical Teaching.' He was filled
with gloom about the state of the world. 'Two daemonic
beings,' he said, '. . . bastards of the "Zeitgeist" and
sophistry, neomania and pleonexia—in German the craving
for novelty and greed—both violent and both cunning in
their different ways, dominate the civilised world. They
are despised by many but idolised by the majority.' 'Both
hide the deficiencies of their true nature,' he went on,
'beneath the ornaments of vain hopes. Under the deceptive
names of industry and enlightenment they penetrate
particularly into the dwellings of the middle class, where
as the offsprings of sophistry they know how to defend and
recommend everything they do. When the justification is
lacking or is insufficient, they appeal to the "Zeitgeist" as
a lawgiver against whom no argument is permitted.' Then
he recalled a conversation some years before with a man
who, commenting on a certain 'aristocratic government,'
had said that, notwithstanding its many virtues, 'it was
bound to collapse because it no longer corresponded to the
spirit of the time.' He said that at the time this remark
appeared nonsensical, but he came to understand it when
he realised the extent to which 'the nihilistic cult of novelty'
was establishing itself in Germany. The result was that the

[1] Cf. H. J. W. Thiersch, op. cit., II, pp. 50–6.

'new wisdom' was directing its venom against classical humanism. His general attitude is summed up in this passage: 'The history of the human race begins with the spring. This we have lost, but its reflection shines even now upon us through the clouds of the present in single rays from classical times. To gather these beams together and, as far as possible, to unite them into focal points of light is the noble task of classical philology. . . . In the spiritual contemplation of the great and powerful world of classical antiquity the noble youth can breathe in the air of a better life than the present can grant and thereby win the power to keep the luring daemons of the time at a distance, to place truth higher than specious brilliance and to value sincerity, even when deceived and misused, higher than the successful lie—in short, even in a sinful and degrading time, to nourish faith in the nobility of man. . . .' 'In our age,' he continued, 'as in every other, what mankind needs above all else is piety. . . . But piety denotes the deep feeling of man's dependence on God, the deep faith in the fatherly control of the world, in moral freedom and in the responsibility involved in our free actions. This faith penetrates the whole of antiquity.' In short, 'classical education is aimed at awakening and consolidating both religious feelings and everything which serves as the basis of a noble and worthy life.'[1]

The enthusiasm with which this speech was acclaimed shows, even if we make allowance for the respect due to such a venerable figure as Jacobs, that it struck a sympathetic chord in many members of the conference. There is, however, the problem of squaring it with certain other addresses which might suggest an opposite impression. One thinks, for example, of Thiersch's paper in the previous year 'On the Relationship between the Common Interests of Humanistic and Industrial Education in Our Time.'

It is wrong, Thiersch maintained, to divide education into two separate categories, humanistic and merely technical. He stressed that in his view things should be so arranged as to give the new industrial class—'the source of

[1] This important speech is reprinted in full in *Verhandlungen*, 1840, p. 8 seq.

progress'—the benefits of humanistic training. He went on to speak thus of the rising industrial class: 'The industrialist in the higher posts, the owner of large concerns, the superintendent of a large trading or bank business, is brought by the nature of his work into contact with all the deeper questions of the time. He moves in circles of world trade and through these in those of politics. Through his speculation he embraces more than one continent and one ocean.'[1] His speech ended with a glorification of the bourgeoisie, 'whose influence and importance is still growing wherever the public order is secure.'[2] 'The citizen of the middle class,' he went on, 'is found in the administration of the affairs of his community. . . . In the meetings of the Estates he takes part in legislation. There is no matter and no task is so high and so difficult that his advice cannot be sought and that it cannot be submitted to him for a decision. If this is so, what we are here discussing is not merely the interest of the middle class but of the whole public weal. To educate him for these affairs, to raise him to the height of his profession and to prepare him for this position in his early years by education and instruction is the task which the age has imposed on its organisers and leaders. Their solution will only be successful in so far as we succeed in raising the middle class itself, by means of a common education both of the future scholar and the future citizen, to the higher standard of understanding and culture which the scholar owes essentially to careful and wise handling in his youth.'[3]

At first sight one is struck by the contrast between this speech and that of Jacobs, by the differences between Thiersch's apparent social confidence and Jacobs' anxious conservatism, his desire to rescue humanity by training people to despise material advances and to submit themselves humbly to the fatherly guidance of their maker. If, however, Thiersch's statements on this occasion are considered in connection with wider aspects of his thought, it will be seen that his position was not really as far removed from that of Jacobs as might appear.

[1] Ibid., 1839, p. 45.   [2] Ibid., 1839, p. 46.   [3] Ibid., 1839, p. 47.

Earlier in this chapter we spoke about Thiersch's attitude to educational questions in the light of the prevailing liberalism of his time. We quoted instances of his outlook with regard to universities. His liberalism was equally evident in his concern for the schools. It was seen, for example, in the Bavarian school-plan of 1829 which was instigated by the king and in the drafting of which Thiersch played a major part. Compared with its predecessor it was far more liberal both in details and purpose. Its character can be gauged from the fact that it was attacked by the conservatives as too liberal and by the radicals as too conservative. Thiersch's position is well illustrated by his reactions to this particular controversy. He spoke against both factions and answered the radicals in a section of his book *On Higher Education* entitled 'On the Alleged Jesuitism and Obscurantism in the Bavarian School-Plan of 1829.'

'The tree of our culture,' he wrote, 'has its roots stretching through all aspects of the past centuries and draws nourishment continuously from everything great, noble and sacred that lies hidden in their womb.' Then, as a true liberal convinced of the desirability of a 'middle way,' he turned angrily against the exponents of a more radical attitude. 'These innovators,' he asserted, 'what else do they want but to tear it up with all its roots in order to erect in its place the sapless, branchless and leafless trunk of their theoretical sham freedom and equality.[1] Vain effort! The oaktree of our revered culture will still be shading and refreshing the generations of a distant future, while they themselves will be brought to ruin by their own delusions.'[2] To the same category, he believed, belonged those whom he called 'realists,' i.e. those who argued that more time should be devoted in the schools to science and its related subjects. One of their leading spokesmen was Oken, at the time professor at Munich. 'Oken's own example,' wrote Thiersch's son, recalling his father's attitude, 'made it necessary to show whither this whole trend was bound to

[1] 'Um an seiner Stelle jenen saft-, ast- und blätterlosen Stamm ihrer pädagogisch-literarischen Afterfreiheit und Gleichheit zu errichten.'

[2] *Über gelehrte Schulen*, III, p. 78.

lead, namely, to materialism and to contempt for all the higher possessions of humanity.'[1] In the same context he quotes a statement of Thiersch: 'It was a question of preserving the sublimity of the human spirit, of keeping it fixed on all that is most high and pure.' Also, Thiersch attacked those who favoured a compromise between classical and 'realistic' education if it meant making serious concessions to the latter. Such a compromise was being advocated about this time in Prussia by Johannes Schulz,[2] and in *On Higher Education* Thiersch devoted a considerable section to attacking it. He even criticised the ancient foundation of Schulpforta in this connection: 'In the ancient Schulpforta, which has been unhinged by this doctrine, mathematics is given such emphasis that classical studies take second place.'[3] The various attacks, mentioned above, on the school-plan of 1829 strongly influenced the king with the result that a new one was issued the following year. This was a retrograde step. Thiersch, who was equally opposed to conservatism and radicalism, was fearful lest it should lead to clerical domination and so undermine the teaching profession. For the moment, however, his energies were diverted elsewhere and he became involved in the problems connected with the insurrection in Greece.

This is not the place to examine every aspect of Thiersch's thought and work, including his struggle against the reactionary partnership of church and state in Bavaria under von Abel, Catholic Minister of the Interior, and its educational repercussions. His defence of academic freedom was undoubtedly liberal in origin and aim, and his views on this subject were shared by wide sections of the middle class. His attacks on the tendency towards a superficial cult of 'general education'—which was being popularised under the influence of Hegelianism in Prussia and which so well served the interests of the 'officials' state'[4]—mirrored the

[1] H. J. W. Thiersch, *op. cit.*, I, p. 304.
[2] Schulz was a senior educational official in Prussia. He expounded his views, for example, in the *Jahrbuch für wissenschaftliche Kritik* and to some extent put them into practice at the time when Altenstein was Minister of Education in Prussia (1817–1838).
[3] *Über gelehrte Schulen*, III, p. 337.
[4] *Cf.* Samuel and Thomas, *op. cit.*, pp. 3–4.

misgivings of many liberal-minded people in these years.
Thus, in opposition to those who regarded the pupil as the
passive recipient of disconnected and ill-digested information, Thiersch said that education should aim rather at
awakening activity in the pupil. He pointed out that, if
a large number of subjects are treated in such a way as to
prevent the pupil from focussing his critical faculties on
any of them, the mind cannot develop and the result will be
an inability to make critical judgments, an attitude of *nil
admirari* to all problems and circumstances. He was convinced that the attempt to give greater prominence to
'realism' in the timetable would lead inevitably in this
direction.

It is, however, important to point out that Thiersch's
denigration of 'realism' in the schools was part of his
defence of an idealism that contained within itself all the
seeds of a conservatism not far removed in its wider implications from that of Jacobs.

At the end of 1831 Count Ludwig von Oettingen-Wallerstein became Bavarian Minister of Education and the
Interior. He was concerned about the situation in the
Palatinate because this region had been deeply involved in
the revolutionary developments about 1830—the Hambach
Festival, for instance, had taken place there. One of the
ways in which the Bavarian government hoped to stem
the tide of 'rationalism'—which it interpreted fairly widely
and in which it saw the *fons et origo* of the revolutionary
movement—was by propagating religious orthodoxy. At
the same time Wallerstein sought to curb the unwelcome
trends by educational reforms. For this reason he asked
Thiersch, whom he greatly respected, to visit the Palatinate
in 1834–36 and to write a report. This was published by
Thiersch under the title *On the Condition of Public Instruction in the Western States of Germany, in Holland and
Belgium.* This appeared in 1839, the year before Jacobs'
speech and in the same year as the important address by
Thiersch to the Classical Philologists, which we have already
summarised. This work is extremely valuable because it
shows with great clarity Thiersch's attitude to certain broad
questions in the period of the earlier conferences of the

Classical Philologists. Particularly significant is the way in which he equates—in a manner that brings him close to Jacobs' position—idealism with the maintenance of the existing order and materialism with the forces directed against it. We shall quote at some length:

The idealistic trend (*ideale Richtung*) regards the present culture as a treasure which has been handed down from past ages by the noblest spirits in word and deed, and it regards its use as bound up with the knowledge of the languages, fortunes and conditions of the times from which it comes. Not only the two ancient classical languages and their literatures fall into this category, but also the oriental languages[1] with the documents of the Bible and the early language and literature of our forefathers and also everything through which we have become what we are—Christianity in its different forms, poetry, the deeper knowledge of history, philosophy, to which must be added our own ancient past and the ideas, convictions and habits on which the social and political systems of the present are based. In short, everything that includes religion, higher education and the state stands on that foundation, draws through its roots, stretching down into the centuries, nourishment and health from it, and it degenerates as soon as these are cut and the present is broken off from the past.

Everything, however, in this traditional field partakes of the nature of the ideal. None of the great things here dominant, neither faith nor feeling for the beautiful, neither the elevation of the spirit nor enthusiasm, neither the recognition of social differences nor respect for their existence, can be counted or measured, and they have their roots nowhere but in the mind, least of all in external considerations. For those people make a great mistake who believe that, for example, religion keeps its position because it is necessary for outward discipline or that respect for existing forms of state survives because these are demanded by general security. If the point comes when the existence and significance of these great things vanish from the spirit of nations, a gentle external push suffices to knock them down as dead and rotten growths.

In opposition to this idealistic trend, in opposition too to the order and culture, life and soul of early European growth and institutions, stands the materialistic trend which is aimed at the acquisition, increase and use of external possessions and at the social importance and prestige conditioned by them. By its very nature it only recognises and can only

[1] Notice that Thiersch associates oriental studies with classical humanism as equally important in this connection—just as they joined hands in these conferences.

regard as valid that which is useful for these purposes, i.e. which increases or gives nobler form to the sum of external possessions. It regards these as all the greater, more important and more desirable because, in the family as also in the state, wealth and importance, and with them power and happiness, are dependent upon them. Since it is concerned only with external and contemporary things, this trend and the outlook that results from it is indifferent to everything which cannot be counted, measured or which cannot be seen or understood as directly useful to its wishes and endeavours. It is on this basis that, from its point of view, the present seems to rest and the structure of the future to have been begun. While up till now it has not sought to destroy the position and importance of the other view, in the most advanced individuals it has now assumed a position which excludes the idealistic trend or is in opposition to it. It regards preoccupation with oriental activity and its languages as a useless activity since everything that is thus brought to light is already available in the simple and comprehensible doctrines of Christianity. Higher education . . . appears to it as merely a game or a foolish pursuit. Interest in antiquity seems to it only a misunderstanding of the age, of its needs and demands, nay, a way of spoiling the youthful mind which is thereby pushed into imaginary circumstances and dangerous dreams and rendered useless for the present-day. In the new order, however, only that is valid which the present has marked with its stamp as the currency of the moment in so far as it is the means by which one can acquire things, such as railways, steam engines, blast-furnaces, sugar factories and so forth or with the aid of applied physics, chemistry and mechanics can prepare the way for discoveries leading to them.

The present culture of Europe is still maintained and protected only by these vestiges of the old possessions of the past, by which it was founded, and by the remains of the desires and convictions nourished by them. If, however, they are completely destroyed by the tide of new forces, surging forward with overwhelming power, let no one doubt that the rest of the edifice will become completely ruined, that the goal of the struggle against all idealistic values in the sphere of culture is barbarism and in the sphere of politics is anarchy . . . it is the process of European world-order reversed, and while this aimed at building up from tradition and at fashioning from it the structure of society and at deriving stability and beauty from it, the present trend sets out to abolish this structure by means of its principles and at the same time to dissolve the whole body of society, and everything that holds it together and feeds it, into its atoms,

i.e. to shifting sand, which is blown hither and thither by all
the winds that blow.

He who strengthens the foundation of the old education
and tries to make its superstructure firm and unshakeable,
who finds in everything great bequeathed by the noblest
minds of the past ages the purest sources of culture for the
spirit, who enthuses youth for all that is noble, sublime and
beautiful, while at the same time sharpening its reason and
quickening its insight, lifting it above ambition for the common
and concrete and raising it up to admiration and the protection
of those possessions on which our life is based—such a man
stands and works for the protection of the highest possessions
moulded by ideals and the traditional culture and the solidarity
of order which rests upon them.

Anyone acts in opposition to this and in the direction of
weakening the ideas upholding it and in the interests of dis-
ruption, who—no matter from what point of view and for
what purpose—undermines the basis on which the culture and
order of Europe rest, or who substitutes another culture
which despises, scorns and attacks the traditional inheritance
of great forbears.   So too does he, in a greater or lesser degree,
who, in the sphere of education and instruction in the training
of the class which in the final resort holds the rudder of states
and of the future in its hands, restricts—by abbreviating or
weakening them—the studies to which tradition owes its
influence, or who pushes them into the background by over-
burdening youth with an excessive number of other subjects
and thus kills interest in them.   Finally, the same is true
also of him who sees in them only a means to certain formal
ends or who regards a little Latin merely as a help towards
certain skills useful to the citizen and aiding material factors.

But on the other hand anyone will play into the hands of
the enemy who does not keep his eye fixed on the manifold
needs of the present, who does not try to satisfy them, who
neglects to take the necessary measures or to foster whatever
can be beneficial for industry, trade and commerce, whether
in elementary education in its various forms and its wide
development, whether in technical or practical instruction.
All this means that we must watch and act with special care
while at the same time endeavouring to protect that fortress
of civilisation, founded on the traditional studies.   Whoever
takes account of both and tries in equal measure to provide
for the studies necessary to the higher learning and the higher
trades that which is advantageous to both and thereby is in
truth the mediator between their antagonisms, will be the
person in whose efforts one recognises the beneficent and

blessed hand, which alone is capable of cultivating the garden of culture and tending its varied harvest.[1]

After the preoccupation with the past in the first part of Thiersch's statement, one is surprised to discover his interest in 'the manifold needs of the present' and in 'whatever can be beneficial for industry, trade and commerce,' although reference was made above to a speech at one of the conferences in which Thiersch spoke equally emphatically of the importance of the new industrial class. This inconsistency is not the least significant feature in this quotation, for it mirrors the situation in which the German bourgeoisie found itself at this time, impatient of the restrictive conservatism of the feudalists and fearful of the 'mob.'

Thiersch was at least as much concerned with the dangers as with the opportunities. He spoke of civilisation as involving a 'recognition of social differences' and 'respect for their existence,' of the bourgeoisie as 'the class which in the final resort holds the rudder of states and of the future,' but his confidence wavered. The growth of industry might open boundless prospects of man's control over nature but Thiersch, and many like him, felt it necessary to weigh the advantages against the dangers of its social consequences, of 'barbarism' and 'anarchy.' For to the bourgeoisie throughout Europe in the eighteen-forties 'the very word "republic" sounded as sinister as the word "soviet" in the years following 1917. . . . Even in 1848 the upper-middle class was convinced that political equality would not only sweep away the advantages of birth and wealth, but would at once abolish private property and lead to the destruction of civilisation.'[2]

This is the perspective in which we have to consider the motives that led Thiersch to attach such importance to the conferences of Classical Philologists. He himself described them frankly in the letter, already mentioned, to Gottfried Hermann, seeking his collaboration. 'There is a general feeling,' he wrote, 'about the weakness of philology that is mainly concerned with matter-of-fact considerations. But

[1] *Über den Zustand des öffentlichen Unterrichts*, I, p. 6 seq.
[2] Taylor (ed.), *op. cit.*, p. 28.

there is no lack of readiness to strengthen this weakness, and our Society claims your sympathy and that of your pupils particularly because it could provide the opportunity to do so. For in the end we work for the same end, and understanding between us about the proper means is, so it seems to me, as easy as the union of our branch of scholarship and of those working on its behalf against enemies which are of equal danger to us all, namely, the ever-growing industrialism and materialism.' It was in this predicament that Thiersch championed idealism as the ally of the existing order and combatted materialism as its enemy.

There were good reasons why this attitude was particularly conspicuous in the case of Thiersch and the Classical Philologists. There was no sphere in which the claims of the bourgeoisie to pre-eminence were more marked than in that of 'culture,' none in which it was more sensitive to its prestige and prerogatives, none in which it was easier to argue that material advance was a secondary consideration since all true values were those of the spirit. Classical humanism in Germany was beginning to serve as a defence of the culture of a property-owning middle class—of 'Bildung und Besitz'—against the rising tide of socialism. It did so increasingly in the sharpening social struggles later in the century and this is one of the striking features of German education in the Wilhelminian era.

CHAPTER III

THE CONFERENCES OF UNIVERSITY TEACHERS OF GERMAN
LAW, GERMAN HISTORY AND GERMAN LANGUAGE
('GERMANISTEN')

Important as were the conferences of Scientists and
Doctors and of the Classical Philologists, it is to those of
the 'Germanisten' that the student of modern Germany
turns with the greatest interest. No debates, not even
the meeting in 1847 at Heppenheim of the parliamentary
opposition of Baden, Württemberg and Hesse, contain such
valuable material as those of the 'Germanisten' for anyone
anxious to understand the climate of liberal opinion in
Germany immediately before 1848. The 'Germanisten'
complete the picture to which the other conferences contribute in their different ways. In particular, they provide
a focal point of the nationalism of the liberal intellectuals
which can be here examined with exceptional clarity and
concreteness. It is true that the crisis in Schleswig-Holstein
intensified the political character of the 'Germanisten'
congresses, as will be shown later, but the developments
at these conferences arose naturally from the general
circumstances of the German middle class.

The suggestion that led to the first of these gatherings in
1846 came from A. L. Reyscher. As he is comparatively
little known it will be necessary to say a few words about him.
In 1829 he became a lecturer in law at Tübingen, being
promoted to a full professorship in 1837. He had already
won the esteem of Jakob Grimm and Mittermaier and was
known through several published works in which he had
argued the claims of German law against those who wished
to retain Roman law as the basis of the German legal
system. Thus, in 1828, he had attacked the protagonists
of Roman law in his book *On the Needs of Our Time in
Legislation*, and five years later appeared his *Symbolism
of Germanic Law*. In this issue, the significance of which
we shall discuss later, an important part was played from
1839 by the *Journal for German Law*, edited by Reyscher

in collaboration with Wilda (of Halle, later of Breslau). The two men had met at the centenary celebrations in Göttingen (where the idea of the conferences of Classical Philologists originated). 'In order to take something permanent home,' Reyscher said, 'from the distractions of the celebrations, I instigated a gathering of the "Germanisten" who in Göttingen had special cause to remember the progress made from there in the study of German law, especially under Eichhorn, as also in other branches of scholarship. About twenty colleagues working in this field were present. I advocated the founding of a journal for German law and it was my wish that a few respected colleagues should direct it. All were agreed about the need, but no one would undertake it till Wilda agreed to share the task with me.'[1] 'The aim of the journal,' Reyscher went on, 'was . . . not merely to provide a meeting-point for investigations in the field of native German law, but also to contribute towards the encouragement of a *national* study of law and thereby to the creation of a *patriotic* (*vaterländisch*) science of law. . . . The specifically national element (*Volkseigenthümlichkeit*) . . . does not consist in a contempt for what comes from abroad, in a failure to recognise the merits of foreigners, and it does not desire the alienation of peoples. We can therefore, without contravening our principles, regard as our own not merely that which has already established itself among us, but we shall also try to incorporate as part of our spiritual possessions all real progress which we perceive in other countries. But how can one value what has been produced abroad more highly than that which is native to one's own country without a closer knowledge of the latter?'[2]

These extracts from Reyscher's memoirs will suffice to indicate the general trend of his ideas shortly before he became involved in planning the conferences of the 'Germanisten.' The plan for the first of these was discussed in some detail by Reyscher and Adolf Schmidt during the summer of 1845. In the autumn of the same year Reyscher tried to arouse interest in the scheme in university circles during a journey through North Germany. In particular, Jakob

[1] *Op. cit.*, p. 89.   [2] *Ibid.*, p. 90.

Grimm was influential in the arrangements for the inaugural meeting, held at Frankfurt-on-Main.

Various considerations determined the choice of place. As a Free City with a great tradition it obviously had many historical advantages for a congress of liberal intellectuals stressing the 'national' tasks of German scholarship.

Other considerations were mentioned by Uhland in a letter in October, 1845, to a correspondent in Frankfurt: 'The only reason why I add my name to the public announcement is in order that in this area sympathy should be shown towards an undertaking which reckons on active support from all German states. It is from this point of view that Frankfurt would be especially suitable for the first "German-isten" conference because of its central position. In a fairly large town the beginnings of such an enterprise are less in evidence; its inhabitants do not need, as in the case of smaller places, to be burdened with accommodation and other claims, and the scholars can devote themselves with greater concentration to their aims because they are less noticed.'[1]

The invitation,[2] published in the German press, began by stating that it was the example set by other academic conferences that had suggested the idea of the proposed congress. 'Natural science and classical philology,' it said, 'have for a number of years found how great are the advantages to be derived from gatherings in which acquaintances are made and ideas collected.' It went on: 'Three sciences, which are closely connected and which in the last decades have been strengthened and supported by each other, desire similarly to partake of the same advantages.' The undertaking was to be essentially national in character. The aim was thus defined: 'Stimulus in the field of scholarship, the making of personal acquaintance and the reconciliation of differences, except in so far as these are necessary in the field of research, will be the aims of the meeting. This is an objective on which agreement is possible even among those who differ in other respects, provided it is

[1] *Ludwig Uhlands Leben*, etc., p. 331.

[2] 'Einladung an die Germanisten zu einer Gelehrten-Versammlung in Frankfurt a.M.,' reprinted in the *Verhandlungen der Germanisten zu Frankfurt am Main am 24., 25. und 26. September 1846*, pp. 5–6.

truth that they seek.' One section of this invitation dealt with organisation: 'The conference itself will decide about the form and method of the discussions and about the question of repeating the conferences after two or three years.[1] Meanwhile it can be assumed that speeches freely delivered from notes (*freie Rede*) and informal conversation will predominate and that lectures read from a manuscript will as a rule be excluded. The question of dividing into several sections will depend partly on the number and inclination of those present, partly on the subjects under review, many of which at any rate will be suitable for discussion in full session. In this respect, following the example of other conferences, we are proceeding from the fact that, while the meeting will be public, active participation will be limited to the circle of those who have demonstrated their contribution to the advance of German scholarship by their writings or in office.' 'It would be too much to expect of a scholars' conference,' it was added, 'that it should set itself the task of visibly furthering individual doctrines or of directly intervening in practical affairs; but we hope for by no means inconsiderable results from our conference if, as is not to be doubted, it is firmly based on scholarly investigation, does justice to the seriousness of the time and fills each individual with the enthusiasm that inspires the whole.' The signatories, seventeen in all, included Arndt, the close associate of Stein, author of famous patriotic songs at the time of Napoleon and a university professor; Beseler, Professor of Law at Greifswald; Dahlmann, Gervinus, Jakob and Wilhelm Grimm, Mittermaier and Reyscher, all of whose activities are described elsewhere; Lachmann, the famous Berlin philologist; Lappenberg, Hamburg archivist, collaborator in the *Monumenta Germaniae Historica*; Pertz, principal figure behind the *Monumenta*; Ranke, the famous historian; Adolf Schmidt, Professor of History at Berlin; Uhland, the poet; Wilda, professor at Breslau, one of the founders in Germany of the comparative history of law. A considerable number of

---

[1] The decision was in fact taken at the second conference in 1847 to hold the next meeting at Nuremberg. This did not materialise, for after the failure of 1848 the *raison d'être* of the organisation, as it then existed, was destroyed.

these men were or had been politically active in the Diets
or were soon to become members of the Frankfurt National
Assembly.

It will be noted that the first sentence of the invitation
acknowledged the debt to the conferences of Scientists and
Doctors and of the Classical Philologists. This was further
underlined by Reyscher when, opening the first meeting,
he said that 'the plan has been worked out with reference
to the statutes of other scholars' conferences . . .'[1] The
influence of preceding congresses is seen in that section of
the invitation dealing with the objectives of the new organisation, in the stress on the importance of social intercourse
as a means of overcoming mutual hostility and cliquish
differentiation. 'We do not want to be merely "Germanisten,"' said Gervinus in the course of a speech in 1847 at
the second conference, 'but also human beings. It would
be superhuman if after the strain of the journey we were
to come here to listen in the morning to long lectures and
then immediately after lunch were to enter into the most
earnest debates. One of the main aims would be lost,
namely, that of quiet discussion and personal intercourse.'[2]
Another respect in which the Scientists and Doctors left
their mark on the arrangements of the 'Germanisten'—as
they had done on those of the Classical Philologists—was,
as the invitation indicates, the intention to make the
meetings discussions rather than a series of formal lectures.
Section 9 of the statutes therefore laid down: 'As a rule the
lectures will not be read from a prepared text. In exceptional cases the chairman can, according to the particular
character of the subject, permit the speaker to read a
prepared text.' As was seen earlier, Oken's wishes in this
matter had more than a mere technical significance. They
arose from his desire, influenced by the changing social and
political needs of his time and class, to transform scholarship
from a narrow academic pursuit into a factor capable of
influencing wider sections of the public. It was this intention of broadening the scope and impact of scholarship on
society that had led the Scientists and Doctors, while
restricting actual participation in the debates to those

[1] *Verhandlungen*, 1846, p. 10.   [2] *Ibid.*, 1847, p. 55.

qualified under the statutes, to admit the public to the meetings. This important principle was followed by the 'Germanisten' and it was formally incorporated in section 2 of the statutes. It is also noteworthy that the 'Germanisten' conferences were to embrace scholars from different, though related, branches of study. Here again the example had been given by Oken's organisation which brought Scientists and Doctors together, just as the Classical Philologists had been meeting in conjunction with secondary schoolmasters and orientalists. It was a far cry from the particularism characteristic of German scholars in the more backward conditions of the eighteenth century to Jakob Grimm's declaration at the 1847 congress of the 'Germanisten' 'that almost all the sciences are connected.'[1] As regards the creation of specialist sections, it will be recalled that Oken had emphasised the need to maintain the importance of the general sessions in order to prevent the fragmentation that might follow from an uncontrolled development of sectional activities. In this connection the statutes of the 'Germanisten' laid down: 'The creation of sections . . . depends partly on the subjects under discussion.' But it was added, no doubt with the example of the Scientists and Doctors in mind, that 'the first and last session will be a general one for all members.' In fact, at the first gathering sections were founded for history, law and language, and in each case the proceedings were published as appendices to the main report. Gervinus described the conferences as 'a federal state of three sections,' and warned against the dangers of allowing anyone of them to develop 'into a state within the state.' 'We in Germany,' he argued, 'must learn how to consult and organise, and it is reasonable for us to exercise ourselves in these small tasks, so that we may acquit ourselves with honour.'[2] An equally striking

[1] Ibid., 1847, p. 64.

[2] Ippel (ed.), Briefwechsel zwischen Jacob und Wilhelm Grimm, Dahlmann und Gervinus, Berlin, 1885, II, pp. 87-8. Gervinus was actually referring to his fear that Ranke's proposal (at the first of the conferences) to form a German Historical Society (cf. Verhandlungen, 1846, pp. 200-1) might disrupt the unity of the conference by giving too great an importance to one aspect of its work. The Society was founded and its statutes discussed, and it was agreed, at the suggestion of Pertz, to make the editing of the proceedings of the old Reichstag the first task. But the political events of 1848-9 intervened and nothing much came of it.

similarity between the 'Germanisten' and their forerunners
is that they shared the belief in the value of changing the
meeting-place from year to year. This feature was mentioned, for instance, by Jakob Grimm when he opened the
1847 conference at Lübeck (where he was again President).
The change of location, he said, would enable Germans from
all parts of the country to attend at least some of the
conferences and it would further help, he added, to destroy
any narrow regionalism that might otherwise characterise
the sessions.[1] This note had been struck by Reyscher at
the very outset of the first congress when, in terms that sum
up the final aim, he spoke of the intention of 'uniting the
scattered forces which are active in the different areas of
Germany on behalf of *German* history and *German* law,
into a great whole for the benefit of scholarship and to the
honour of our common fatherland.'[2]

In his speech as President at the opening of the first
conference Jakob Grimm tried to steer the discussions away
from politics.   'As far as politics are concerned,' he declared,
'let them be kept away from our gatherings, which have
no decisions to make about them, although it will be natural
and inevitable in the sphere of history, law and even of
language to tackle and handle problems bordering on the
field of politics with scholarly discipline.'[3]   His own pro-
nouncements on the same occasion involved matters that
were implicitly or explicitly political.   For example, he
had just declared: 'There is no place in our gatherings for
that difference between north and south Germans, which
one can call foolish and insulting, which only makes sense
in so far as it may sometimes be advantageous to compare
north German faults and virtues with those of the south.
. . . No such difference can crop up in our midst, just as
none of that unhappy confessional conflict must enter our
conference which in our time confuses men and turns
them against each other.   Our forefathers were Germans
before they were converted to Christianity. . . . No confessional cleavage must be allowed to pollute a great people
which is once again conscious of itself and desires to maintain

---

[1] *Verhandlungen,* 1847, p. 3.   [2] *Ibid.,* 1846, p. 9.
[3] *Ibid.,* 1846, pp. 17–18.

its position.'[1] The situation was well described by Beseler:
'In spite of the careful delimitation of the aims, it was soon
clear that the nationalist tendency in the political movement of the time was bound to find expression here. Uhland,
on the evening of the opening meeting, spoke in quite the
right terms when in a powerful speech he pointed to the
pictures of the emperors in the Römer[2] which, he said,
would leap from their frames and mingle with the members
in order by their mere glance to animate and also to bridle
their enthusiasm.'[3] No doubt, this helps to explain the
more spontaneous and natural character of the proceedings
of the 'Germanisten' as compared with the other conferences.
A letter written by Gervinus during the first meeting reflects
the difference: 'At all previous gatherings of the Scientists,
Philologists, etc., the boring reading of manuscripts, the
vagueness of the meetings, has displeased me. I like
associations, like those in England, which set themselves
definite aims to achieve in practice.'[4]

Even more marked was the contrast in this respect between
the 'Germanisten' and the 'German Societies' of an earlier
period.   These had drawn together certain—predominantly
bourgeois—elements whose desire was to collaborate on a
more collective basis in the defensive needs of the time
against Napoleon. First suggested by Arndt,[5] they were
designed, in the words of Meinecke,[6] to create 'a network
of public societies throughout the whole country with the
aim, wherever possible, of getting hold of every citizen
and filling him with activity.' It was, as Meinecke points
out, a great jump 'from the restrictiveness of bourgeois
life hitherto, from the traditions of a loyal and narrow
performance of duty within a society divided up into
estates and with little community of interests beyond these
limitations.' These societies, however, were characterised
by a sentimental adulation of the past and by a hazy
emotionalism. Arndt himself had stressed the need to

---

[1] *Ibid.*, 1846, p. 17.   [2] The Town Hall at Frankfurt-on-Main.

[2] *Op. cit.*, p. 54.   [4] Quoted in Ippel, *op. cit.*, II, p. 88.

[5] In his *Entwurf einer teutschen Gesellschaft*, 1814.

[6] *Die Deutschen Gesellschaften und der Hoffmannsche Bund*, Stuttgart,
1891, p. 10.

cultivate in them what he pretentiously called 'the direct strength of life and the great power of the soul.' Such an ideal was not likely to impart a clear sense of direction even when adorned with wordy tributes to Germanism and the national character. Furthermore, these societies operated for the most part amid the pettyfogging conditions of German small-town life of the time. The actual realisation of the ideals envisaged, however vaguely, was impossible without a more fully developed community spirit, and this had yet to be formed.

It is sometimes customary to regard the period between 1815 and 1848 as dominated by the features usually associated with the German term 'Biedermeier'—by a turning away from public affairs, a withdrawal from the responsibility of social and political decisions to more private and domestic spheres of interest. This was in certain respects true of the years immediately after the defeat of Napoleon. As Rudolf von Delbrück summed up from his own experience, 'the interests of the educated circles in public affairs in the eighteen-twenties had been extremely scanty. The great excitement which seized the nation to its very foundations in the years 1806–15 had been followed by a weary relaxation.'[1] But from about 1830 a different trend can be observed. The July revolution in France, the insurrection in Belgium, the Polish rising, the outbreaks of revolutionary activity in different parts of Germany were among the factors that, to quote Delbrück again, 'awakened the interest in politics and made day-to-day events the object of conversation.'[2] From 1840 onwards public interest increased very considerably in the political problems of the time. In Baden, for instance, there was a marked rise in the decade before the revolution of 1848, seen in the heightened interest in the debates of the Diet, in the rising circulation of existing journals and the creation of new ones, in the greater attention in the press to political issues and the interest shown by the public in the personalities and activities of the members of the Diet.[3] Even in a relatively

[1] *Lebenserinnerungen 1817–1867*, Leipzig, 1905, I, p. 38.
[2] *Ibid.*, p. 38.
[3] Cf. Karl Ruckstuhl, *Der badische Liberalismus und die Verfassungsfrage 1841–43*, Basel, 1911, p. 136 seq.

backward state like Mecklenburg public opinion showed signs of greater liveliness at this time.[1] 'The national movement of the intellectuals who cultivated and developed the idea of national unity and power,' it has been stated, 'begins first in the eighteen-forties to influence the masses, certainly under the influence of the national threat of 1840[2] but certainly connected also with the economic and social advance.'[3] 'Thus, with the growing wealth and extending trade,' said Engels, 'the bourgeoisie soon arrived at the stage where it found the development of its most important interests checked by the political constitution of the country. . . . At the same time the extension and consolidation of the Customs Union, the general introduction of steam communication, the growing competition in the home trade, brought the commercial classes of the different states and provinces closer together, equalised their interests, centralised their strength. The natural consequence was the passing of the whole mass of them into the camp of the liberal opposition, and the gaining of the first serious struggle of the German middle class for political power. This change may be dated from 1840, from the moment when the bourgeoisie of Prussia assumed the lead of the middle-class movement of Germany.'[4]

The growing political consciousness of the bourgeoisie expressed was reflected in the desire to relate theory and practice. Some of the famous and most productive university teachers of this period were active politicians either in the Diets, the Pre-Parliament or the Frankfurt National Assembly. Mittermaier, to take one example, was a professor at Heidelberg from 1821; in 1831 he was elected to the Second Chamber of the Baden Diet, was its President in 1833, 1835 and 1837, in 1848 became President of the Pre-Parliament and a member of the National Assembly where nearly one in five members was a school or university

[1] Cf. Adolf Werner, *Die politischen Bewegungen in Mecklenburg und der ausserordentliche Landtag im Frühjahr 1848*, Basel, 1907.

[2] The 'war scare' of 1840, provoked by the fear of French interference with Germany's western frontier.

[3] Meinecke, 'Zur Geschichte des älteren deutschen Parteiswesens,' in *Preussen und Deutschland*, p. 154.

[4] *Op. cit.*, pp. 6–7.

teacher.[1] Thirteen years before the first of the conferences
of the 'Germanisten,' Dahlmann wrote in *Politics*: 'The
gap between knowledge and ability, between the power
of understanding and strength of character, has become
enormous. Are those who read and teach most about
bravery really brave? Do they really make sacrifices for
their country? . . . Where is disease more at home than
among scholars? Where is there a more frequent lack of
that powerful balance of spiritual and physical activity
which distinguishes the successful human being?' Five
years after this book was published appeared the fourth
volume of Gervinus' *History of German Literature* (1840)
with a dedication to Dahlmann, in which Gervinus declared:
'Our poetry has *had* its time; and, unless German life is to
stand still, we must attract the talents, which now have
no aim, to the real world and the state, where a new spirit
must be poured into new matter . . .'[2] One thinks too
of Theodor Mundt's conception of 'immanence,' which, he
said, 'is the term applied to that ethical education of
character which from an attitude demands at the same time
deeds, from thinking demands being and from action
demands uncompromising publicity.'[3] He criticised the
literature of his time for having separated itself from the
'centre of national life where it should stand'[4] and, as has
been said, proclaimed the doctrine of literary popularity
'understood as accommodation to matters of national
importance.'[5] Similarly Gervinus lauded Georg Forster
as a man 'who found the difficult transition from the idea
to the deed, from principles to practice, from knowledge to
action.'[6]

[1] 19·6 per cent. (as against a mere 6·2 per cent. in the National Assembly
of 1919.) For full details cf. L. Rosenbaum, *Beruf und Herkunft der
Abgeordneten zu den Deutschen und Preussischen Parliamenten 1847 bis
1919*, Frankfurt a.M., 1923.

[2] I have examined Gervinus' views on some aspects of German literature
at greater length in a paper, 'Gervinus and the Age of Goethe,' to appear
in the *Publications of the English Goethe Society* for 1950.

[3] *Aesthetik. Die Idee der Schönheit und des Kunstwerks im Lichte
unserer Zeit*, Berlin, 1845, p. 17.

[4] *Ibid.*, p. 2.

[5] C. P. Magill, 'The German Author and His Public in the Mid-Nine-
teenth Century,' in *Modern Language Review*, October, 1948, p. 498.

[6] From his essay on Forster in the latter's *Sämmtliche Werke*, VII, p. 10.

The increasingly political attitude to scholarship was seen particularly in the sphere of history and law, both of which had an obvious and direct bearing on the political issues in which the bourgeoisie was most deeply involved. It was here that it could best justify its demands and formulate the changes which it desired. Writing in 1832 from Florence to a friend in Germany with reference to his plans for a later work,[1] Gervinus said that its aim would be not merely to interest scholars but also 'the greater mass of people by its popular presentation,'[2] and this was also the intention of his short-lived *German Yearbooks*.[3] In 1840 Rotteck made a characteristic generalisation when he said that the tendency was for historians to present their material in more popular form in order to achieve as wide an influence as possible and 'thereby to give public opinion a democratic (*freiheitlich*) character.'[4] In the preface to his *World History* Rotteck had described the study of history as 'the only remaining organ for proclaiming the truth'[5]—referring to the absence of democratic institutions as a means of public discussion and propaganda; and Welcker could describe this work as a major contribution towards awakening public opinion to ideas of spiritual and political freedom.[6] In the dedication to Gervinus, Jakob Grimm described his *History of the German Language* as 'political through and through.' There is considerable truth in Schnabel's statement[7] that, while conservatives argued that political ability was inborn and inherited, the liberal intellectuals maintained that it could be acquired by the study of history. Among the impressions of the 'Germanisten' conferences recorded by Karl Hegel (son of the celebrated father) was the scanty attention paid to the

---

[1] The reference is to the *History of German Literature*.

[2] Cf. Rudolf Unger, 'Gervinus und die Anfänge der politischen Literaturgeschichtsschreibung in Deutschland,' in *Nachrichten von der Gesellschaft der Wissenschaften zu Göttingen*, Berlin, 1935.

[3] Cf. Gervinus' 'Einleitung in die deutschen Jahrbücher,' in *Ges. kl. hist. Schr.*, pp. 326-7.

[4] 'Betrachtungen über den Gang, Charakter und heutigen Zustand der historischen Studien in Teutschland,' in *Ges. u. nachg. Schr.*, Pforzheim, 1841-3, I, p. 376.

[5] Quoted in Boehn, *op. cit.*, p. 338.

[6] Cf. *ibid.*, p. 338.   [7] *Op. cit.*, II, p. 201.

exponents of history as a 'pure' science, like Pertz and
Ranke.[1] Certainly most of the 'Germanisten' would have
rejected as outrageous Lord Acton's notion that historical
studies 'ought to be all but purposeless . . . pursued with
chastity like mathematics.' As regards law, Gaupp spoke
for many when at the first meeting of the 'Germanisten' he
declared that this study too should be made to serve as
'a prophet of the future.'[2]

This attitude was hardly consistent with the basic doctrines
of Savigny and the Historical School, though some of the
liberal intellectuals were or had been closely associated with
it. Their ideas, for example, differed from those of the
poet Eichendorff, a conservative nobleman, whose political
essays,[3] like much of his poetry, bewailed the faithlessness
of those who break the 'natural' bonds of life. An
amusing satire on the liberal professors from a conservative angle is contained in Eichendorff's short story
The Professor. It describes some liberals who meet in an
inn 'Zum Goldenen Zeitgeist.' Eichendorff symbolises the
professor's political theorising in a journey, accompanied
by the author, on a winged horse to the Brocken. The
author comments: 'I was quite unaccustomed suddenly
to be raised right above all existing things between heaven
and earth and to hover in empty nothingness.'

The two camps had a different approach to the fundamental question as to whether the citizens of a state had the
right to determine and change the pattern of the legal
system.[4] The Historical School denied this right on the
grounds that, historical evolution being an organic process
subject to its own laws, it should develop at its own speed
and without interference. This view was part of the conservative reaction against the impact of the French Revolution and it was aptly characterised by Marx as seeking to
justify the misery of the present by the misery of the past.
Generally speaking, the liberals ranged themselves against

[1] *Leben und Erinnerungen,* Leipzig, 1900, p. 131.

[2] *Verhandlungen,* 1846, p. 125.

[3] Cf. for example, 'Der Adel und die Revolution' and 'Preussen und
die Konstitution,' in *Sämtliche Werke* (ed. Kosch and Sauer), X.

[4] This was denied by Savigny in his essay *Über den Beruf unserer Zeit
für die Gesetzgebung* (1814).

this conception and they had on their side the important thesis of Thibaut who (in his essay *On the Need for a General Civil Code for Germany*, 1814) argued that people had the right to 'make' the laws under which they live. 'But if we now consider law,' he wrote, 'in its inner being and essence, the conviction will thrust itself even on the most impartial of people that a wise, carefully thought out, simple and clever (*geistvoll*) legal code is the very thing that is indispensable for the strengthening and inspiration of the citizens of Germany, in order that a powerful counter-weight may be provided for the political fragmentation of the country and all the petty irritations inseparably con-nected with it, and we cannot escape the conclusion also that as a rule no single ruler will be in a position to have such a legal code drawn up by his servants.'[1] The contro-versy often found expression in arguments about the nature of the 'Volksgeist' or spirit of the nation. The difference in attitude has been summed up thus: 'There were those who held themselves justified in concluding that what mattered above all was the cautious, almost imperceptible further development of existing society in the old estab-lished forms. Others thought that it was precisely these that ought to be pushed aside as remnants of a completed age in order to provide new vessels . . . for quite new forces.'[2] Some words applied to Dahlmann are true of the liberal intellectuals of the period as a body: 'The "spirit of the nation" (*Volksgeist*) means to him the self conscious-ness of the bourgeoisie, whose expression was public opinion.'[3] Dahlmann, however, was too conservative in his liberalism to provide a sharp contrast with the Historical School. In this respect Gervinus is a better example. 'The impeded instinct of our national life,' he wrote in 1847, 'can be heard in all these resorts to absolutism, aristocracy, classes, past forms of state and old forces; it is heard in the teaching of the Historical School.' What

---

[1] *Über die Nothwendigkeit eines allgemeinen bürgerlichen Rechts für Deutschland*, p. 34.

[2] Lina Kulenkampff, *Der erste Vereinigte Preussische Landtag 1847 und die öffentliche Meinung Südwestdeutschlands*, Basel, 1912–13, p. 19.

[3] Hermann Christern, *Fr. Chr. Dahlmanns politische Entwicklung bis 1848*, Leipzig, 1921, p. 78.

was indispensable was 'an instinctive development of the national life, avoiding dangerous political experiments as much as excessive caution,' and 'no one could be less qualified to lead us' towards this goal 'than those men of the Historical School.'[1]

The political character of the conferences of the 'Germanisten' was mirrored in the discussions regarding the German language. It would be a great error to regard them as signifying merely an academic interest in problems of philology.

At the time of the Napoleonic invasion it had been widely recognised that the preservation of the German language was a weapon in the struggle against the French. Even the old historian Heeren, rooted in the eighteenth-century Enlightenment, had insisted on this in his pamphlet *On the Means of Preserving the Nationality of Conquered Nations*.[2] 'Thus, the preservation of nationality,' he wrote, 'depends specifically on the maintenance of language,'[3] and he added: 'Respect for one's mother-tongue, however, reveals itself in the fact that one uses it wherever one can. Voluntary use of a foreign language, when it is not necessary, always denotes a momentary alienation of nationality. The German who speaks French or English ceases meanwhile to be a German, as far as that is possible.'[4] Ideas such as these found expression in an organisation called the Berlin Society for the German Language,[5] founded in 1811.

Jakob Grimm himself was made an honorary corresponding member of this body in 1816 and two years later of the Frankfurt Scholars' Society for the German Language. But he was convinced that in their attempts to purify the language these societies went much too far,[6] and in a letter to Benecke in 1818 he entirely supported his correspondent's

---

[1] *Die preussische Verfassung*, p. 102.

[2] Written in the spring of 1810 and first published in Perthes' *Vaterländisches Museum*, Hamburg, 1810.   It is reprinted in Heeren's *Historische Werke*, Göttingen, 1821, II.

[3] *Ibid.*, p. 21.   [4] *Ibid.*, p. 22.

[5] Interesting in this connection is Otto Schulz, *Die Sprachgesellschaften des 17. Jahrhunderts. Vorlesung am Stiftungsfest der Berlinischen Gesellschaft für deutsche Sprache*, Berlin, 1824.

[6] Cf. Karl Franke, *Die Brüder Grimm. Ihr Leben und Wirken*, Dresden and Leipzig, 1899, p. 83.

disparaging remarks about the Frankfurt organisation.
He had stated his own attitude in 1812: 'Every individuality
should be kept sacred, also in language. . . . The Danes
are beyond reproach in that they try to counter the open
penetration of German words and phrases; but it is foolish
to believe that a million and a half people can cut themselves off from the irresistible pressure of a closely-related
language spoken by thirty-two millions.'[1]

Grimm opposed those who thought it desirable or possible
to remove all foreign elements from the German language,
but he asserted the obligation to avoid the use of foreign
words as far as practicable. This was a matter to which
he attached so much importance that he devoted a section
of his Presidential address to it at the first of the 'Germanisten' conferences. It would be wrong, he argued, to try to
purify the German language by violent means and impossi-
ible to prevent the penetration of words from the old-
established languages of neighbouring peoples. 'It is a
sin,' he declared, 'to use foreign words where good or even
better German ones are available as a result of irresponsible
ignorance of our native use of language. In short, the
task is to keep our language pure and to recognise its pure
usage rather than to purify it in an arbitrary manner and
extend its usage without proper authority.[2]

This argument indicated the need for a precise and
scholarly analysis of the state of the German language from
which people could learn what forms were valid and what
were not. Grimm was as a matter of fact already engaged,
in collaboration with his brother, on the famous dictionary,
and Wilhelm Grimm discussed this at a later session of the
same conference. 'We want,' he reported, 'to depict the
language as it has itself developed in the course of three
centuries, but we draw our material only from those in
whom the language manifested itself most vitally.'[3] The
aim was 'to refresh the feeling for the life of the language'
and again to awaken 'feeling for its purity.'[4] As in earlier
statements he opposed 'strait-laced purism'[5] and stressed

---

[1] In the *Allgemeine Literatur-Zeitung*, 1812.

[2] *Verhandlungen*, 1846, p. 14.　　　　[3] *Ibid.*, 1846, p. 118.

[4] *Ibid.*, 1846, p. 121.　　　　[5] *Ibid.*, 1846, p. 123.

the mutual indebtedness of one language to another. But
he urged the necessity to cultivate the native features of
the German language as part of the respect due to German
nationhood. 'Indeed, I must confess,' he commented,
'that in this place, from the respected speakers at this
gathering who have the glory and fame of the fatherland
very much at heart, I have heard more foreign words than
is tolerable.'[1] It should be added that for Grimm the
Dictionary stood for something far more important than
the mere printed word. He felt it to be a co-operative
enterprise in the hands of those who cherished the interests
of the nation, a means of bringing them together to activity
in the national cause. Thus, writing to Uhland in 1839,
he described it as 'work which by its very idea is a general
patriotic undertaking.'[2]

When Grimm had finished speaking Gaupp underlined
the significance of these remarks by placing them in a wider
perspective. Goethe, he pointed out, had said that it was
in vain that the Germans hoped to become a nation. 'This
was spoken in a sad time,' he said, 'and it must not be allowed
to make us downcast. We will attain that aim too if we
concentrate all our powers on making our circumstances
ever purer and more perfect. But the poet also adds: "But
for that reason you can better develop your humanity."
In these words the fairest and highest task is given to us—
the development of noble humanitarianism on the basis of
deeply-felt nationality. Yes, it was especially for that
purpose that the Germanic peoples have become the bearers
of modern world-history.'[3]

The approach of the 'Germanisten' to certain questions of
language illuminates their attitude to law.

The problem was similar in so far as the main point at
issue was the advantage of German law over Roman law.
Reyscher's view of the problem, in the period immediately
before the plan of the 'Germanisten' conferences was proposed, has been summed up in these words: 'As the task
of contemporary "Germanisten" he saw the gradual liberation from foreign law through the more careful cultivation

---

[1] *Ibid.*, 1846, p. 123   [2] *Ludwig Uhlands Leben*, etc., p. 281.
[3] *Verhandlungen*, 1846, p. 129.

of the law which in the most varied forms had sprung up on German soil and of the living law of the present-day as well as through preparation of a national code of law as defined in the journal founded by him. In order to advance this task it seemed to him that a personal meeting of "Germanisten" was . . . particularly desirable.'[1] Thus the problem itself had been instrumental in bringing the conferences into being, and some of the most important debates were devoted to it. Of course, it was only reasonable to discuss the question at all if it was agreed that men had the right to change the laws of their society.

In the debates about law we see clearly the way in which the growing nationalism of the bourgeoisie was intimately bound up with its movement for political emancipation.

The problem of law had been raised by Grimm in the opening session of the first meeting, significantly in the same speech in which he had dealt with language. In his personal development the study of language and law were closely interwoven, and he had early thought of writing a book on Roman law.[2] The incorporation by Napoleon of Hesse in the kingdom of Westphalia resulted in the introduction there of the *Code Napoléon*; this so upset Grimm and his brother that they gave up the study of law—Wilhelm for ever, Jakob returning later to German law. Jakob was drawn closer to literature and philology as an alternative corresponding to his patriotic interests. As he said in his inaugural lecture in Berlin, in German language and literature he found consolation. He had begun his study of German legend and mythology when Savigny's essay set forth the programme of the Historical School. 'It was poetry,' he said in 1829, 'that led me back to old German law.'[3] This link was seen, for example, in his essay 'On Poetry in Law' (1815),[4] to which Uhland paid a tribute in the first 'Germanisten' conference as among the first of a

---

[1] *Op. cit.*, p. 99. This quotation is taken from the narrative which links together the various items from Reyscher's memoirs.

[2] Cf. 'Rede auf Wilhelm Grimm,' in *Kleinere Schriften*, I, p. 167.

[3] Quoted by Rudolf Hübner, *Jacob Grimm und das deutsche Recht*, Göttingen, 1895.

[4] Published in second volume of the *Zeitschrift für geschichtliche Rechtswissenschaft*.

series of essays marking the first stage in Grimm's intense study of German law.[1]

'German law,' Grimm declared to the 'Germanisten,' 'is in a peculiar position. If one considers its scope, it is not a general science, in the same sense as language, but it is restricted . . . to isolated doctrines which have still maintained themselves side by side with Roman law, which has flooded the whole surface of our legal system.'[2] As in the case of language Grimm was against artificial and impracticable 'purism.' 'Violently to tear out Roman law,' he said, 'after it has for long been accepted among us and our whole legal outlook has been closely interwoven with it, seems to me a monstrous piece of purism, as intolerable as were an Englishman to act as if it were possible to expel Romance words from the English language and to keep only those of Germanic origin.'[3] The better alternative, he thought, would be to rescue through careful historical research those elements of German law that had become submerged in course of time and thus to prepare the way for a revision of the whole legal code.   *89665*

The direction of his thought was thus not wholly consistent with that of Savigny. Since the thinkers of the Historical School denied that citizens, in Savigny's phrase, were 'qualified' to impose their will on legal institutions, their appeal to historical continuity could lead only to an affirmation of Roman law. Grimm's idea was that research should be directed to the task of rescuing the vestiges of German law, building them into a unity and applying them as far as circumstances permitted. The result would be, he thought, to fill in the gaps left in the system of Roman law, even to provide a substitute for it in those respects in which it no longer corresponded to the needs of the age. Those who held this view, he said, were the allies 'of those among modern historians who regard it as desperately necessary to construct politics from history.' With such writers he disparagingly compared those whom he described as 'the more passive historians,'[4] who for all their learning merely plough up the soil with old tools. This stricture has a

---

[1] *Verhandlungen*, 1846, p. 15.   [3] *Ibid.*, 1846, p. 15.

[2] *Ibid.*, 1846, p. 16.   [4] *Ibid.*, 1846, p. 16.

bearing on the Historical School, even though Grimm always proclaimed his indebtedness to Savigny: 'I confess myself your pupil, and yet the pupil has remained very unlike his teacher, has become different from him in almost every respect.'[1] It would be hard to find a more concise illustration in any of these conferences of the desire to relate scholarship to political tasks, to make it serve the needs of the nation. It was the importance of concentrating on this aspect that led to the decision to exclude, with two exceptions, teachers and upholders of Roman law from the conference. 'If one were to invite the "Romanisten,"' Reyscher said, 'this would not merely contradict the purpose of the conference, but they would constitute the majority and our national interests would be lost in this gathering just as up to now they have been lost in the sphere of scholarship as a whole.'[2]

'Our law,' Mittermaier bluntly declared, 'stands in opposition to life, to the national consciousness, to the needs, customs, attitude and ideas of the people.' 'Nationality,' he added in the same speech, 'expresses itself in its purest and best form in the law of the people.'[3] He proceeded to develop his argument in a way that throws light on another type of objection to Roman law. 'This Roman law,' he said, 'is a masterpiece of analysis and perspicacity.'[4] But its virtues were also its weakness. 'What made Roman law great,' he explained, 'is the work of jurists. Jurists created it. The frightful logic with which certain legal principles are carried through, that is the main thing that is decisive in Roman law.'[5] He went on: 'What is our German law, was it created by jurists? It has grown from the people, custom has created. it . . . It is for this very reason that in German law we find that all statutes are consistent with the conditions of life . . . while in Roman law only this frightful logic determines everything.'[6]

This argument against Roman law that it was 'fixed' by jurists was important and characteristic. It arose from the

[1] From his tribute to Savigny on the jubilee of his doctorship, 'Das Wort des Besitzes,' in *Kleinere Schriften*, I, p. 114.

[2] *Verhandlungen*, 1846, p. 83.   [3] *Ibid.*, 1846, p. 64.

[4] *Ibid.*, 1846, pp. 64–5.   [5] *Ibid.*, 1846, p. 65.

[6] *Ibid.*, 1846, p. 65.

desire of the bourgeois thinkers, as the intellectuals of a
rising class, to free law from the shackles of the existing
state, to bring it more into line with changing needs. Jurists,
as professional bureaucrats, were part of the apparatus of the
state with which the liberal movement was in conflict.
One recalls in this connection the statement of Thibaut,
who combined advocacy of a 'German' code of law with
the reservation that it should not be drawn up on behalf
of a prince by his servants. Conservative thinkers, on the
other hand, stressed that it was important to keep law in
the hands of 'experts,' who could see all points of view
whereas, as Rehberg put it, 'men with a definite job in
middle-class trade'[1] only perceived their own limited
interests. Beseler's comments are worth mentioning here.
He declared that, though he had always been a supporter
of Roman law, he realised the force of some of the arguments
against it, and he stated his misgivings in these terms:
'Now the question arises whether it is necessary for a
people, in the further development of economic and political
circumstances, to be completely excluded from participation
in making and exercising law and . . . whether such a
separation is healthy.'[2] It was this very feeling that led
Mittermaier to emphasise the 'rigidity' of Roman law, its
inability to adapt itself to new social and economic requirements.

It is interesting to note the examples that Mittermaier
used to prove his case. Many of them concerned problems
of inheritance with special reference to the security of
family relationships. There is a clear connection between
the impatience of these men with existing legal provisions
and the concern of the bourgeoisie for property. This was
the age in which Hegel attributed to property a quasi-
metaphysical sanction, declaring that appropriation was
the essence of personality and in which Brüggemann in 1847
described property characteristically as 'the foundation
and corner stone of all morality and all personal liberty.'[3]
'Think further of the relations,' Mittermaier argued,

[1] A. W. Rehberg, *Die Erwartungen der Deutschen von dem Bunde ihrer
Fürsten*, Jena, 1835, p. 47.

[2] *Op. cit.*, pp. 46–7.   [3] *Kölnische Zeitung*, 1847, No. 14.

'between a father and mother, consider from this angle the whole rigidity of Roman law. . . . Take a case which I know from among my neighbours, a case in which the father has run away and left the wife in the lurch and in which the wife alone administered all the property of the children. Now the father returns and asserts his claim to the children's property. The mother has no claim to it, she who alone protected, advised and cared for them. . . . I ask you, what would be the result if in this case one were rigidly to follow the law as it stands and if in the most important matters where the well-being of the children is concerned the father alone were to decide and the mother on the other hand were not to be heard? Does that correspond to the needs of the people?'[1] He went on to deal with property rights more explicitly and also of problems arising out of second marriage, seeking to show that in these respects Roman law contradicted the real interests of the people. Similarly, and very interestingly, he referred to the law of contract. Here again he was concerned with the security of inherited rights of property, and he gave some examples. 'I know a case,' he said, 'in which a man in North Germany has given his estate over to his son. The father has in addition a sickly and weak daughter. Therefore, in handing over the estate, he made the condition that the son, who had received the property, should maintain the sister during her lifetime and pay her a monthly income. The father died, and then it was pointed out that the daughter unfortunately had not signed. There was a great conflict. It was laid down that contracts are not valid for third parties. Does this entirely un-Germanic principle not lead to terrible consequences?'[2] He concluded his speech with the remark: 'Gentlemen, it is time to conjure up the spirit of German law, the spirit of the German nation, in order that it may penetrate our law.'[3]

On much the same lines was the speech of a professor named Christ. 'A law,' he said, 'can only be a national law, for law is nothing other than the customs of a people which assert themselves in the sphere of law. These customs

[1] *Verhandlungen*, 1846, p. 66.   [2] *Ibid.*, 1846, p. 69.
[3] *Ibid.*, 1846, p. 71.

are the actual law, and from this point of view law is nothing but the revelation of nationality, the incarnation of the life of the soul, as it reveals itself in a particular nation.'[1] 'Just as it is true,' he continued, 'that the law of individuality runs through the whole of moral and physical nature, it is equally true that every person is by nature different in body and in his way of thought and action; it is equally true again that every nation in its deepest foundations has an essentially different individual form and therefore possesses forces which operate differently in the creation of law.'[2] In nature he claimed to find a powerful argument in support of this idea of inherent national differentiation, and he rounded this section of his statement with the assertion: 'In this sense, I say, all law is national. Every nation will and must have law that is different from that of every other nation.'[3]

We shall refer later to certain important implications of this kind of argument, but meanwhile we must quickly summarise another significant legal discussion. In the second of the conferences the question of a unified code of law for the whole of Germany was debated. In some respects this was related to the discussion just mentioned, but emphasis was transferred from the advantages of German over Roman law to a consideration of the benefits of a common legal system for the German nation. The debate followed a proposal from Gaupp who, in the spirit of Thibaut, declared that the time had come to reorganise law on a national basis. The extent to which members felt that this problem affected their existence is seen from the reception given to Gaupp's suggestion which, as Karl Hegel records, evoked 'a storm of enthusiasm.'[4]

'Our beautiful Germany,' declared Gaupp, 'has so much that uplifts the heart and soul that we can be proud to possess this fatherland. It is true that much is still lacking . . . namely those things that are necessary to arouse and strengthen the spiritual unity of the country. It is with joy that we have welcomed in Lübeck men from all regions of Germany. East, west and other parts have sent repre-

---

[1] *Ibid.*, 1846, p. 74. [2] *Ibid.*, 1846, p. 74.
[3] *Ibid.*, 1846, p. 74. [4] *Op. cit.*, p. 131.

sentatives here. We welcome them all as Germans, sons of a single stock.'[1] Then he went on to lament, despite this sense of common nationality, the absence of a system of law valid in all parts of the country: 'It is true that our native dwelling has many mansions which are beautiful and benign. . . . But has every one of us the right to settle in each one of these? Is each of us able at will to become a citizen of one of these? In other words, have we really got a German civil code?'[2] He drew attention, for example, to Article 18 of the charter of the Confederation which stated that every German could acquire property in any state. The problem for him was to implement this principle in practice. He referred with approval to the Customs Union, to a recent proposal by the Prussian government regarding the introduction of a common currency and to a recent suggestion by the government of Württemberg about a unified legal code—all admirable in his view as far as they went.

This speech was strongly supported in particular by Mittermaier who followed. As to the means of achieving this objective, he stressed especially the need to combine scholarship with practical experience in planning it. His suggestion was that a commission should be appointed to sift and examine all the relevant material. It is significant that he recommended that the example of England should be followed, for England was a country to which, owing to its more advanced economic and political development, the German liberals—especially after the success of the Reform Bill of 1832—tended to look for precedent and guidance. 'What explains the excellence of British legislation?' Mittermaier asked, and he answered by saying that in England commissions were appointed in which theoretical knowledge and practical experience could support each other. As to the composition of this commission, he emphasised that 'men of scholarship' should sit side by side with the practitioners of law. It is a good thing, he commented, 'when practice and theory combine to achieve a common goal.'[3]

---

[1] *Verhandlungen*, 1847, p. 201.   [2] *Ibid.*, 1847, p. 201.
[3] *Ibid.*, 1847, p. 206.

The reasons which Mittermaier put forward to prove the need for a unified code of 'German' law are worth noting because, though they add nothing new to Gaupp's arguments, they were more precise and concrete. 'Yes, gentlemen,' declared Mittermaier, 'I think it would be magnificent if every member of the smallest state in the German Confederation could say: I belong to this or that state, without having to fear that he might be expelled by all other German states.'[1] He developed Gaupp's statement: 'If we had a unified code of law like other nations, how splendidly industry, commerce and trade of all kinds would develop, whereas now we have to struggle against a mass of wearisome formalities and official obstacles when business overlaps from one state into another.'[2] His argument demonstrated most clearly the link between his ideas and the interests of a trading and commercial bourgeoisie in the period of developing capitalism in Germany. He quoted, for example, the case of a manufacturer known to him. This man lived in one state and wanted to establish a factory in another offering greater opportunities for business. This man—'moderate in his political views, an enemy of all revolutions'—had asked for Mittermaier's advice as to his position. The latter explained to him that the laws of the German Confederation laid down that a person had the right to acquire and possess property. His friend, however, pressed him for a more precise definition and was told that, while he could set up his factory in another state, the police there could turn him out whenever they wished— and so he decided to let the matter drop. 'Therefore,' commented Mittermaier amid loud acclamation, 'I demand this German code of civil law in the name of German industry.'[3]

A different aspect of law, trial by jury, also received considerable attention from the 'Germanisten.' This question was raised at the 1846 meeting, both in the general assembly and in the law section. It was then decided to set up a commission to enquire into the pros and cons. This met under the presidency of Mittermaier—a

[1] *Ibid.*, 1847, p. 204. [2] *Ibid.*, 1847, p. 202.
[3] *Ibid.*, 1847, p. 205.

great believer, as we have seen, in commissions—who reported on its behalf to the conference in the following year, where the matter was hotly debated.

It is true that there were dissentient voices but, significantly enough, they were those of the two 'Romanisten' present by special invitation. Freiherr von der Pfordten was opposed in principle to the whole scheme, mainly on the grounds that it would subordinate justice to passion and the domination of the masses.[1] Wächter too had sufficient misgivings to place him really in the opposition. His argument relied largely on the idea that trial by jury infringed the natural contract uniting prince and people.[2]

Wächter's fear that too much might be attempted too quickly proved groundless, for the report of the commission was essentially moderate in its recommendations and implications. The main contention was that trial by jury protected the individual from arbitrary condemnation. 'Trials by jury,' Mittermaier said in presenting the report '. . . under suitable conditions give citizens the greatest security against groundless accusations,'[3] and he added that special importance was to be attached to the public character of the proceedings, which was indispensable for their full success.

The question of trial by jury was, as it were, the microcosm of the wider problem of democratising the whole institution of government. It was typical of the conference that the broader aspect was not discussed as if it were a timeless abstraction but in its historical development and context. The most important single speech on this theme was that by a Hamburg professor (Wurm) on 'The National Element in the History of the German Hansa' in 1847. It is noteworthy that the case for parliamentary democracy and constitutional rights was most powerfully presented by a man from one of the most developed centres of German trade and that it was inextricably interwoven with considerations about the extension of commercial interests.

'My point of view,' he declared, defining his approach, 'is the national one.' He posed the question: 'From this

[1] *Ibid.*, 1847, p. 148.   [2] *Ibid.*, 1847, p. 123.   [3] *Ibid.*, 1847, p. 91.

standpoint what was the German Hansa, what ought it to become in accordance with its nature, what could it become in the given conditions of Germany, what ought it to have become according to the wishes of every patriotic German?'[1] Briefly, his argument was a lament for the fact that 'the national foundation, instead of growing ever more secure, was narrowed down . . .'[2] He regretted the failure of the old Reich to transform the Hansa into a truly national organisation and to establish a navy strong enough to develop and protect Germany's trading interests. One result, he said, was not only 'that England would no longer tolerate our supremacy in trade,' but also that she imposed her superiority on Germany. The Reich had both failed to prevent this and also to safeguard German trade by a tariff barrier (and he pointed out that Ranke had drawn attention to the existence of such a project in 1522). The chance, then missed, could have been made good, he asserted, in 1813 when Stein assured delegates from the Hansa states that 'it was the intention to arrange a tariff at all the frontiers of Germany.'[3] This approach to history was characteristic of the debates in general. The speaker was not concerned with historical analysis as an academic exercise, but his account of the past was at the same time a discussion of the needs of his own time. His partisanship was even clearer in what he said about the German Confederation. This had become the object of widespread criticism among German liberals for a variety of reasons— on the grounds that it impeded trade through its lack of unity, that it was a league of princes, that it stood in the way of liberal reforms and that it hindered the growth of national power. 'But in this new confederation of the German nation,' he asserted, 'what prospects were opened up for the realisation of those common interests which the Reich had once so totally neglected?'[4] His criticism of the Confederation was the voice of a bourgeoisie whose economic interests were clamouring for organisation and development on a national scale. 'It is true,' he went on, 'that it is concealed in the protocols of the assembly of

[1] Ibid., 1847, p. 5. [2] Ibid., 1847, p. 5.

[3] Ibid., 1847, p. 15. [4] Ibid., 1847, p. 13.

the Confederation, but in those protocols you find that the towns proposed and recommended measures that could give us unity; unity in the German postal system—it is a scandal that we have not got it!—national German consulates in foreign countries—it is a scandal that we have not got them!—a German flag. . . . But the German sea-trade went unhonoured and unprotected by the council of the German Confederation as in the past by the throne of the Emperor and by the high council of the Reichstag. Finally it was even officially declared that the council of the Confederation, i.e. the only organ which the whole German nation possesses to represent its common interests, was not the right place and authority to bring about an agreement about commercial interests.'[1]

The failure of the old Hansa, he argued, had not been due only to the fact that its organisation had not been actively and energetically developed by the Reich. It had been connected also with its own internal character and so he passed on to questions of constitutional development. He criticised the old Hansa for its lack of a democratic basis: 'In the councils of the Hansa not all towns were represented, the smaller ones were dragged along by the more powerful ones. . . . Only the senates of the towns were represented, and one would have considered it not much better than high treason if a senate had wished to submit the decisions of the Hansa council to the body of citizens for ratification.'[2] This brought him to the question of the Customs Union. He spoke in much the same terms as those used at the liberal congress at Heppenheim in the same year, where it was maintained that the Customs Union should be given a more democratic character by the creation of a Customs Union Parliament. This was later established by Bismarck (after the Austrian war), whose method was always to make such concessions to liberal opinion as were necessary to help him consolidate the power of a reactionary monarchy. 'The German Customs Union,' said Wurm, 'whose national element will rejoice the heart of every German, is only a forerunner, as the Hansa was— a forerunner of what is to come, of the completed develop-

[1] *Ibid.*, 1847, pp. 15–16.　　　[2] *Ibid.*, 1847, p. 16.

ment and of a truly national foundation.'[1] How was this achieved? 'If you ask,' he stated, 'how Germany is to find development necessary for effectively safeguarding her commercial affairs, we are struck above all by the fact that the present deficient organisation of the Customs Union will remain a necessity so long as it is a league of governments and not of the German nation.'[2] He went on to widen his case into a demand for constitutional democracy—'speak of what the future is to bring. . . . I speak of the German parliament.'[3]

It was, however, in the discussions about the crisis in Schleswig-Holstein that the nationalist element in the conferences of the 'Germanisten' found its most forthright expression. The affair made a powerful impact on the meetings and gave them a unifying theme of dramatic urgency. As Beseler put it, 'if history, law and language are the subjects of our debates, one can say that all three are almost equally involved in the Schleswig-Holstein affair.'[4]

The duchy of Schleswig, to recapitulate the background of the crisis, had been regarded as part of Denmark since the early part of the eleventh century. Holstein had been German in character since the early twelfth century. Both Schleswig and Holstein were predominantly German in population. In 1460 the duchies were declared inseparable in perpetuity, Schleswig remaining in the kingdom of Denmark and Holstein in the Holy Roman Empire (later becoming part of the German Confederation). A special problem was created when the Danish royal house was threatened with extinction, as the heir to the throne (who succeeded in 1848) was childless. The question of the future of the duchies was complicated. In Schleswig the female line of the ruling house of Holstein-Glücksburg was the legitimate succession, but in Holstein, where Salic Law was valid, the succession lay with the house of Augustenburg. The obvious solution would have been the separation of the duchies, if it had not been for the ruling in the fifteenth century forbidding this. National feeling ran high in

[1] *Ibid.*, 1847, p. 18.   [3] *Ibid.*, 1847, p. 19.
[2] *Ibid.*, 1847, p. 19.   [4] *Ibid.*, 1846, p. 19.

Denmark, Germany and the duchies. The Danes were anxious not to lose Holstein, while the inhabitants of the duchies, backed by wide sections of German opinion, were determined that Schleswig should not remain under Denmark. The affair reached the dimensions of a crisis when the King of Denmark, Christian VIII, published the famous 'Open Letter,' stating that he proposed to regard the Danish law of succession as valid also for Holstein. At this point the German Confederation intervened with a protest 'instead of declaring itself non-competent as was its custom whenever it was necessary to defend the interests of the German people against princely violence.'[1] 'It was the first occasion since it came into being,' wrote Karl Hegel, 'that the German Diet gave joy to the German people.'[2] By 1848 the situation had ripened into revolt and war (in which Prussia took part), but the details of this development after the close of the second 'Germanisten' conference need not concern us.

The tension created by the crisis dominated the first of the conferences, which opened less than three months after the 'Open Letter' of the Danish King (8th July)—this 'infringement of German legal rights,' as Welcker rightly described it[3]—and only about a week after his reply (18th September) to the statement of the German Diet. This was not the first time that the problem of the duchies had been acute. 'The difference,' said Michelsen, 'is merely that now the German national consciousness is awake, that the feeling for law finds stronger expression, whereas at the beginning of the last century there was a political stillness of the grave.'[4] Speaker after speaker, including some of the most famous liberal intellectuals of the time in Germany (Dahlmann, Welcker, etc.), rose to defend the German claim to the duchies, combining meticulous scholarship with political partisanship. They could speak with a good conscience, for here was an issue in which the national cause was legalistically the right one. Thus Jaup could declare in this connection that 'it is a characteristic German

---

[1] Mehring, *Karl Marx*, English translation, 2nd impression, London, 1948, p. 166.

[2] *Op. cit.*, p. 131.   [3] *Verhandlungen*, 1846, p. 32.

[4] *Ibid.*, 1846, p. 52.

quality to respect and do honour to law wherever it exists.'[1]
Furthermore, it was an issue in which the German Confederation, so often and so correctly criticised by liberal
opinion for its failure to champion national interests, had
intervened, even though it did little more in the first instance
than lodge a rather tame protest. Reyscher went so far as
to urge that the conference, after taking a vote, should
publish its decision 'like a jury,' which would have meant
that it should for all practical purposes constitute itself as
the voice of the nation and assume functions of the parliament of the German people. Members were not unaware
of the implications, and Reyscher's proposal was turned
down. Its rejection, however, caused a measure of ill-feeling
which almost disturbed the harmony of the gatherings.[2]

The issue of the duchies was debated in these conferences
to a great extent in legalistic terms, but the passion which
was aroused indicated the extent to which the material
interests of the bourgeoisie were involved. Lappenberg's
declaration that 'all our spiritual forces are set in motion'[3]
should not lead us to disregard in this connection the
importance of the trading and maritime value of the duchies.
This was reflected, for example, in Dahlmann's share in the
discussion. The Schleswig-Holstein affair led him to think
—like Arndt about the same time[4]—in terms of the creation
of a Scandinavian League, to which the German Confederation should ally itself, as a defence alike against Russia and
'the commercial despotism of England.'[5]

[1] *Ibid.*, 1846, p. 38.
[2] It was opposed by Pertz and Mittermaier on the grounds that such
a conference had no right to pronounce a verdict on what was a legal
issue under dispute and that such action might jeopardise future academic
congresses (*ibid.*, 1846, p.p. 50–1). In the *Allgemeine Zeitung* of 22nd
October, 1846, Jakob Grimm published a short report on the conference
(reprinted in his *Kleine Schriften*, VII, p. 573 seq.). The way he spoke
about the episode irritated Reyscher, who replied (anonymously) in the
same paper on 30th October and to this Grimm in turn replied on 13th
November. Grimm discussed it also in a letter to Dahlmann (dated 7th
November, 1846, reprinted in Ippel, *op. cit.*, I, p. 517). Cf. also Reyscher,
Erinnerungen, p. 102 seq., his comments in *Zeitschrift für deutsches Recht*,
10, p. 505 seq. and Adolf Schmidt's remarks in *Zeitschrift für Geschichte*,
8, p. 186 seq.
[3] *Verhandlungen*, 1846, p. 112. For his attitude in its wider context
cf. E. H. Meyer, *J. M. L. Lappenberg. Eine biographische Schilderung,
mit Benutzung von Briefen und Tagebüchern*, Hamburg, 1867.
[4] Cf. his *Erinnerungen aus dem äusseren Leben*, Leipzig, 1840, p. 360.
[5] Quoted by Christern, *op. cit.*, p. 210.

The conferences of the 'Germanisten,' as will be evident from this analysis, reveal in a particularly striking manner the interpenetration at this period of liberal and nationalist values. It has been pointed out that among the reasons for this conjunction of liberalism and nationalism was the fact that after 1815 the German bourgeoisie was fighting against what amounted to an international conspiracy of the forces of reaction. The political struggle of the progressive forces in German society against princes and aristocracy, whose future depended on the preservation of dynastic interests and therefore of the multitude of states, was fully justified in regarding itself as patriotic and in basing its campaign on appeals to national unity. The great majority of progressive thinkers—that is to say, of those engaged in the movement of political liberalism against the obscurantism of a dying aristocratic order— were nationalist in their outlook. At the same time, however, there were important contradictions both in their nationalism and their liberalism.

It was shown, for example, that the 'Germanisten' were enthusiastic about the idea of a unified code of law for all Germany. In an age in which many of the most progressive trends were towards the ideal of the democratic nation-state, this was clearly a demand which no body of German liberals could in the circumstances fail to press. It was a vital weapon in the battle of ideas against dynastic interests which alone stood to gain from the political fragmentation of the country. It was therefore, to say the least, incongruous that a speaker should have advanced the following argument, amongst others, to demonstrate its advantages: 'That arrangements of this kind, such as particularly a German code of law, civil rights and rights of domicile, are very desirable, that the disadvantages of the political fragmentation of Germany can only be removed by increasing the spiritual unity, no one will doubt; and the effects of fostering the German national consciousness will serve to protect and strengthen the German governments.'[1] Again, in summing up the views of the commission of trial by jury, it was stated as one of the advantages that its

[1] *Verhandlungen*, 1847, p. 204.

verdicts would carry the greatest confidence and effectiveness and so heighten people's faith in their governments.[1] In the discussion on Schleswig-Holstein it was stressed that 'fortunately in this case law coincides with the advantages of Germany, with the interests of the German Confederation and also of the German governments.'[2] Consistency was hardly a virtue to be attributed to intellectuals whose concern for freedom was qualified by their anxiety to maintain cordial relations with a quasi-feudal state determined to make the smallest possible concessions to parliamentary democracy.

More striking were the contradictions in the nationalism of some of the 'Germanisten.' National unity was essential for economic progress. In this period nationalism was among the most powerful ideological weapons of an ascendant class against the organised forces of social, economic and political stabilisation. But it was not long before the bourgeoisie's dislike of an international settlement in a conservative sense began to be qualified by its fear of the international forces of proletarian revolution.

We can conveniently summarise a general development by reference to the poet Tieck. He had begun as an enthusiastic devotee of the French Revolution, grew alarmed about the jacobin extremism and proclaimed[3] a middle position directed alike against the tyranny of the princes and the power of the masses. It is entirely correct to say of Tieck that he 'is basically typical of the German bourgeois. If he comes to boast of the benefits of the monarchy, it is because it appears to him to be the best safeguard of this bourgeoisie, which he considered "the marrow of every state".'[4] 'From 1793 he begins to feel the original value of everything Germanic at the same time as he reacts against the levelling cosmopolitanism of his time.'[5]

We noted in an earlier section that Christ, for example,

---

[1] *Ibid.*, 1847, p. 91.　　　　　　　　[2] *Ibid.*, 1847, p. 50.

[3] Cf. for example, his comedy *Der gestiefelte Kater* (1797).

[4] Robert Minder, *Un Poète Romantique Allemand: Ludwig Tieck (1773–1853)*, Paris, 1936, p. 263.

[5] *Ibid.*, p. 259.

defended his demand for a revision of the legal code on the grounds, amongst others, that law must be in line with the 'consciousness of the nation' (*Volksbewusstsein*), the 'life of the nation' (*Volksleben*), the 'customs of the nation' (*Volkssitte*).[1] It would, however, be wrong, despite the resemblance between this type of argument and certain questionable features of later German thought in the age of expansive nationalism, to attach much significance to single statements such as these in the absence of further evidence.

At the beginning of the first meeting Jakob Grimm had asked: 'What is a nation (*Volk*)?' He defined it as consisting essentially of people speaking the same language. This, he asserted, was the proudest and most innocent boast of Germans, pointing towards a future 'when all barriers will fall and when it will be recognised as the natural law that it is not rivers or mountains that constitute the dividing lines between nations, but that language is the only factor that set a limit to a people that has penetrated over mountains and rivers.'[2] This could serve as a paraphrase of Dahlmann's statement that 'race can mean more than the state,' and it represented a directly political application of Grimm's philological studies. This feature was marked in other ways in his statements about language at the 'Germanisten' conferences—in his concern, for example, for the preservation of German in Belgium and Holland[3] (at a time when these areas were being regarded as so vital to German commercial interests).[4] In 1848, discussing the importance of the mother-tongue in the dedication to Gervinus of his *History of the German Language*, he could qualify his regret that Lorraine, Alsace, Switzer-

---

[1] *Verhandlungen*, 1846, pp. 74–5.   [2] *Ibid.*, 1846, p. 11.

[3] Cf. *ibid.*, 1846, p. 13.

[4] The Dutch prevented Germany from having free use of the mouth of the Rhine and at the same time the North German ports refused to join the Customs Union.   This meant that the Rhineland lacked a customs-free connection with the North Sea.   Hence, for example, Hansemann (in his pamphlet *Über das Verhältnis des Zollvereins zu Belgien*) urged a rapprochement of Germany and Belgium.   At the same time Camphausen, Hansemann and Mevissen—among the leaders of liberalism in the Rhine-land—were closely interested in the plan for a railway linking Cologne with Antwerp *via* Aix-la-Chapelle (cf. on this point, *Kölnische Zeitung*, 1847, No. 293).

land, Belgium and Holland were 'estranged' (*entfremdet*) from Germany by the thought that the separation was not 'irrevocable.'

One of the reasons that led the 'Germanisten' to give attention to this question was the emigration of large numbers of Germans before 1848 to America. 'The great value,' said Grimm, 'of the possession of the language and poetry of their native land must be particularly felt by those who are moved to divest themselves of it. I am thinking of the German emigrants who for the past ten years have been crossing over to America in an uninterrupted stream. Would it not be practicable and valuable that measures should be discussed and implemented in order to preserve among them, in the new home of their choice, their traditional language and thereby a warm connection with their motherland?'

Grimm's proposal bore fruit to the extent that in 1846 the 'Germanisten' discussed the setting-up of a commission. One of the leading spokesmen on behalf of this idea was Lappenberg who argued about the need for a 'Society for the Preservation of German Nationality.'

He opened his case by recalling how the events in Schleswig-Holstein had moved all hearts and he urged that steps should be taken to prevent the recurrence of a similar situation. It was in this connection that he made the remark, quoted earlier, that the seeds of German nationality should everywhere be defended against those who would destroy them. Describing to his audience 'how German language and German scholarship had to struggle in Belgium' and also the alleged hostility to German culture of Slavs and Magyars, he went on to say that there were tens of thousands of Germans outside Europe. Stating that England had preserved her colonies through 'the indestructible sense of nationality, by language and the conception of law,' he asked whether Germany would and could not do anything to ensure her possession of her sons in America, Australia, Asia and Africa.' He thought that practical details should be worked out by a commission. This was duly established 'in order to try to define the means which German scholarship could use to influence

the preservation of German nationality and language outside the states of the German Confederation.'[1]

Its report was read and discussed at the following conference. It drew attention approvingly to the activity
of a Dr. W. Stricker, author of a work about 'the dissemina-
tion of the German people over the earth' in 1845 and the
originator of a journal *Germania* devoted to the history and
interests of Germans abroad, and to a weekly recently
started under the editorship of one Fr. Haas under the title
General Emigration Paper.[2] Collaboration was suggested
between the annual conference of 'Germanisten' and
missionaries and ships' chaplains, and it was urged that the
conference should encourage sound German teaching
abroad by ensuring the employment of good teachers and
the dispatch of suitable literature. It was also proposed
that emigrants should be presented with souvenirs of their
native land, that they should be kept in touch with other
Germans in the area of their destination and that the
growth of societies abroad should be stimulated under an
effective central organisation at home.

We may be inclined to treat with derision the way the
'Germanisten' sublimated this question into one of far-
reaching ideological dimensions, and we are likely to sym-
pathise with Dahlmann who, giving the short answer to
those who obscured the simple issue, said that anyone
leaving Germany had to pay the price and that was the
surrender of German nationality.[3] This should not deter
us from taking proper cognisance of the discussions about
emigration with special reference to the political attitudes
involved and to some of the wider implications. For
example, the report spoke with praise of a decree of 11th
June, 1847, of the King of Bavaria, 'who anticipating our
wishes, has made it known that the agencies for emigration
to North America are only to give permission to people
whose outlook justifies the expectation that . . . they
will do all in their power to see that over there Germans
will come together with Germans.'[4] It implied, that is to

---

[1] For Lappenberg's speech cf. *ibid.*, 1846, p. 112 seq.

[2] *Die Allgemeine Auswanderungs-Zeitung.*

[3] *Verhandlungen,* 1847, p. 47.   [4] *Ibid.,* 1847, p. 34.

say, opposition to those whose political radicalism ranged them in opposition to the rulers of the German Confederation and was the decisive factor in persuading them to emigrate. This section of the report, in other words, could only mean that the 'Germanisten' were ready to leave to the state authorities the decision as to which people were fitted to carry Germanism abroad, and that they would rest content with the elimination of politically radical elements. Moreover, underlying the general approach was the emergent conception of ethnographic Germanism, of the 'Volksdeutsche.' This idea was to play an increasingly prominent part as German nationalism passed over into its power-political phase later in the century. The 'Volksdeutsche,' as A. J. P. Taylor has remarked,[1] were an invention of 1848. Here, on the eve of that year, we find German intellectuals coming as near to this conception as was possible without explicitly formulating it.

Clearly the 'Germanisten' were treading on dangerous ground. Even Jakob Grimm let fall remarks which may appear disquieting in the light of later German history and ideas. After asking, in the same context, whether steps should not be taken to link Germans abroad with their homeland, he likened their settlements to colonies, pointing out that Greek colonies had been a means of establishing and preserving Greek language and culture. He compared Germany in this respect to 'a powerful plant rooted deep in Europe,' scattering its seeds over the world. Thus in this conference the theme of emigration was closely connected with that of colonisation. One of the most forthright speakers on the latter subject was the historian Stenzel, professor at Breslau from 1820 and by this time best known through his *History of Germany under the Franconian Emperors*, a man in whom Ranke found 'a spirit of genuine and warm devotion to the state and its princes.'[2] 'The subject of colonisation,' he argued, 'is not quite as unimportant as it appears at first sight.'[3] His speech was largely devoted to a discussion of the benefits which ensued from

[1] *Op. cit.*, p. xxi.

[2] Ranke, *Neue Briefe*, Hamburg, 1949, p. 285.

[3] *Verhandlungen*, 1847, p. 171.

'the great spreading of Germanism in the eastern areas.'[1]
Ludwig Konrad Bethmann—a close acquaintance of Jakob
Grimm and Dahlmann (his teachers at Göttingen)—was
concerned with the same part of the world. His collaboration in the *Monumenta Germaniae Historica* had taken him
in 1844 to Italy and thence to Greece and Egypt. To the
'Germanisten' he proclaimed his belief that Germany had
carried out a historical mission in the east, declaring that
her destiny called for still greater acts in the future. 'A
high spirit,' he said, 'to which Germany owes much, turned
her eyes to the east.'[2] 'It is primarily,' he maintained,
'a question of Asia Minor, where once towns lay side by
side in a veritable garden, and of Syria, the land where milk
and honey flowed. Now they are desolate and full of
ruins. But why should not German colonies, like the
Greek colonies of old, be able to create better conditions
there once more?'[3] He tried to show that the obstacles
sometimes mentioned (climate, etc.) were not insuperable.
'The German,' he asserted, 'who goes to the east will find
that he can live there more easily and longer as a German
than he who emigrates to America. It is true that it is no
use for people to go there as individuals. They must go
there as an organised colony, held together in a single plan
and under a single leadership, like the colonies of the Greeks
and the first groups who went from England to America.'[4]
Germans taking up residence abroad, he claimed, should
regard themselves as 'advanced posts' of Germany and he
thought that they would inevitably extend and become
'bearers of culture.' His ideas could hardly be described
as modest, for he said that he envisaged 'an uninterrupted
chain (of colonies) from Transylvania, through Thrace and
along the Danube to its mouth, which is now closed to us
by the Russians . . . into Asia Minor and Syria.'[5]

Of course, such conceptions were the expression of
emotional attitudes rather than of concrete schemes for

---

[1] *Ibid.*, 1847, p. 179.   [2] *Ibid.*, 1847, p. 181.

[3] *Ibid.*, 1847, p. 182.   [4] *Ibid.*, 1847, p. 183.

[5] *Ibid.*, 1847, p. 184.

dividing up the world. Taken by themselves they might mean much or little. The most that can safely be said is that they might seem to represent a trend of ideas which subsequent German thought and practice have made only too familiar. At any rate they awaken the suspicion that the outlook of the German intellectuals was entering a critical phase, and our task in the next chapter must be to seek for further evidence to contradict or confirm this view.

CONCLUSION

THE CRISIS OF GERMAN NATIONALISM

In our analysis of these various academic and scientific conferences we have been discussing different aspects of the development of liberalism and nationalism in the decades before 1848. It remains to sum up the tendencies which appear to emerge from our examination and the direction in which they were leading. These were related as the outcome and expression of a clearly-marked social process, and they were characterised by certain common objectives and a mutual indebtedness. It would be misleading to consider the meetings of the 'Germanisten' except in connection with those of the Scientists and Doctors and of the Classical Philologists. The 'Germanisten' are both the consequence and the climax of a development that began with the Scientist and Doctors. Our summary could therefore most suitably take the form of an investigation of what concretely the 'Germanisten' congresses produced.

In the conferences of the Scientists and Doctors one looks in vain for any unqualified profession of faith in the revolutionary task of science in society. We were able to quote a passage in which one member referred to the manner in which science had changed society by sweeping away the vestiges of feudalism—but, turning to his own time, he anticipated that the benefits conferred by science would best be safeguarded under the protection of the princes. In such a view we lack the revolutionary verve which would have been indispensable to carry the German bourgeoisie to victory in 1848. Underlying the conferences of the Classical Philologists we found, together with a sincere belief in the contribution of liberalism, the notion that idealism had to be mobilised against materialism—against science—in defence of the existing state against the impact of revolutionary movements from below. These are particular manifestations of the way in which the middle class in Germany in the first half of the nineteenth century began to flinch from the revolutionary consequences of its own ambitions as soon as it began to assert itself. This in itself might have been harmless enough, but there was always the danger that the situation might foster more dangerous illusions than that perfection had existed only in the past and that the present was a debased and degenerate age. For the German bourgeoisie with its growing trading and manufacturing interests had a compelling reason to concern itself with the present and future, to seek to justify them and its own role in the years to come. There was at least the possibility that some sections might discover other and more dynamic forms of inward compensation for the social stresses and hindrances of outward reality, that it might find them in arguments passing beyond the natural concern for political unification in quasi-mystical notions about the expansive claims of Germanism—as happened in the conferences of the 'Germanisten'—and then, under the added pressure of the market, formulate them in power-political terms.

It may seem a far cry from the frightened escapism and timorous conservatism of some of the Classical Philologists to the beginnings of the ideology of modern 'Weltpolitik.' A careful examination of German liberalism before 1848 shows how close in reality was the connection between these apparently opposed trends. It is illuminating, for example, to compare the position reached by Gervinus, a prominent member of the 'Germanisten' and a man whose general outlook was strikingly characteristic of the central stream of pre-1848 German liberalism, with that of Thiersch.

In his praise of Forster, Gervinus had stoutly championed scientific empiricism against idealistic arguments,[1] stressing the importance of what elsewhere he called the 'healthy practical direction of our understanding to that which lies at our feet.'[2] By 1846 he had so far recoiled from the implications of his earlier attitude that he could declare: 'Right at the very core of our own culture lie naturalism and deism, supported and encouraged by philosophy, natural science and history and by the most powerful

[1] Cf. Gervinus' essay on Forster in the latter's *Sämmtliche Schriften*, Leipzig, 1843, VII.

[2] 'Einleitung in die deutschen Jahrbücher' (1835), reprinted in *Ges. kl. u. hist. Schr.*, Karlsruhe, 1838, p. 326.

weapons of the spirit. No matter how noble this culture may appear in its healthy state, the result is that everything around it begins, as it were, to be worm-eaten by atheism, by a corroding hatred among men, by the negation of all religious feeling and its escape into soulless speculation. And now people in this camp are preparing for a campaign of propaganda which has the aim of raising the whole mass of the most common people philosophically to spiritual equality with the higher classes in the same way as it seeks in the spirit of communism to enhance their material possessions. It does this by undermining every prospect of an after-life and every consolation of the poor and oppressed in order to compel them to despair of this life and to destroy what exists in order to build something better.' 'Once already,' he continued bitterly, 'we have seen the fanaticism of dry reason in its frightful effects in the midst of a revolution then in its prime, and among ourselves its undermining consequences are starting to be felt, though we are still very far removed from attempts at actual revolution. These are the circumstances in which we find ourselves. Their influence is striking deeper every day. They threaten prematurely to destroy at the very core all the gains of our spiritual culture, to ruin morality and to unhinge the whole state and national life. No one in authority seems to gauge the danger or to be willing to sense the approaching evil, until it has grown to such dimensions that we stand baffled and helpless. Into this dangerous situation there now comes this church movement which, if it is correctly handled by princes and people, can like a saving angel draw us back from the abyss.'[1] The reference is to the German-Catholic movement, originating in 1844. What appealed to Gervinus in it was the possibility of a form of Christian reunion on a national-German basis, a spiritual alliance capable of counteracting the onslaughts of 'communism' and materialism.

Some months after this pamphlet was written—in the year of the second of the 'Germanisten' conferences—Gervinus became involved in the plans for the creation of the *Deutsche Zeitung*. This was as much a natural outcome

---

[1] *Die Mission der Deutsch-Katholiken*, Heidelberg, 1846, pp. 47-8.

of the meetings of the 'Germanisten' as these marked a
further stage in tendencies already apparent in their pre-
decessors in other fields of scholarship. This is why a
statement of the aims and motives of this paper, as far as
possible in the words of those who were instrumental in
launching it, furnishes a natural conclusion to our evidence.
The preceding chapter showed that the emotional nationalism, which began to assume striking form among the
'Germanisten,' had yet to find expression in power-political
terms. This is what the original prospectus of the *Deutsche
Zeitung* provides. If the conferences of the intellectuals
from 1822 demonstrate some of the quantitative changes
in the growth of nationalism in Germany before 1848, this
definition of the objectives of the *Deutsche Zeitung* reveals
a vital qualitative transformation.

On 9th December, 1846—less than three months after
the first congress of 'Germanisten'—Gervinus wrote to
Dahlmann from Heidelberg to discuss certain organisational
aspects of the paper. He thought it better, he explained,
to establish it in the south-west, instead of Berlin as originally
intended. He reported that Mittermaier, Mathy and Zittel
had discussed with members of the liberal opposition in
Baden the plan of creating such a journal. Dahlmann had
earlier expressed his alarm about the supposed extremism
of the Baden liberals and so in this connection Gervinus
hastened to assure him that they intended 'to make a clean
break with radicalism.'[1] 'At the same time,' he went on,
'it was decided that it was not to be merely a paper of the
Baden opposition but a national German journal. Here
in the small circle of those commissioned to take further
steps in the matter the idea has very quickly taken shape
of summoning together all those forces in Germany which
could be used for a dignified discussion, based on solid ideas
and moderate in form, of the sufferings of the age and their
cure. The extremes in the Chamber, like Hecker, took no
part right from the beginning and it is Mittermaier's view
that they should not be associated with the plan.'[2]

In short, it was to bring together people from all parts of
Germany, to serve as a central organ of moderate liberalism

---

[1] Ippel, *op. cit.*, II, p. 292.　　　　[2] *Ibid.*, p. 292.

—to fulfil a task similar to that to which the conferences of the 'Germanisten' aspired. It is clear from Gervinus' letter that Mittermaier was the main figure behind the plan, the man 'who actually controls it and who says that he prepared the way for it already in Frankfurt.'[1] The reference is to the first of the 'Germanisten' conferences. Moreover, Mittermaier's idea, assuming that these conferences were to be held annually, was that they should form the 'central point' of the new venture.[2] As Gervinus went on to explain, Mittermaier thought that with its nation-wide connections the organisation of the 'Germanisten' could provide the necessary correspondents and valuable stimulus. Some people wanted to make a start in July, but others felt that it would be better to delay it for a year 'in order to use Lübeck (i.e. the second "Germanisten" conference) and the journey thither as an opportunity for verbal contact and discussion.'[3]

These details are sufficient to show how closely the plan for the *Deutsche Zeitung* was bound up with the gatherings of the 'Germanisten.' There is no need here to follow the rest of the correspondence, except to say that on 4th February, 1847, Dahlmann—who had been proposed as editor—informed Gervinus that, while he might contribute in an advisory capacity, he would not take any direct part in the scheme. He thought it premature, but it is clear too that his suspicions about the supposed radicalism of some of those involved had not been allayed. The result was a bitter letter from Gervinus on 5th May, 1847. What is the use of complaining about the situation, he asked, and about the lack of an effective journal if one is not willing to take steps to put it right? At the moment action was more important than excessive caution. In the circumstances there was no alternative but for Gervinus to take over the editorship, and the first number appeared on 1st July, 1847. Already in May a preliminary announcement, written by Gervinus, had been issued, setting forth the character and aims of the new paper. It will be more valuable to quote from the draft which Gervinus

[1] *Ibid.*, p. 292.   [2] *Ibid.*, p. 293.   [3] *Ibid.*, p. 293.

sent to Dahlmann in a letter dated 11th January, 1847.[1]

This began by saying that despite discouragement progress had been made in Germany and that there was good reason to believe 'that it will also in the future be our lot to maintain this progress, to achieve the advantages of a political revision without violent movements, wisely to learn from the sufferings and errors of foreign countries and gradually, following the path of legalism and through the power of the spirit, to attain what other nations have achieved by means of sudden attacks and by violence.'[2] It would be hard to find a more exact definition of the ideals of the intellectual middle class in Germany at this time, with its belief in the methods of constitutional procedure, the rejection of revolutionary action and—one recalls Thiersch's glorification of the 'ideal'—the sustaining power of the spirit. He added, reflecting the growing impatience of the bourgeoisie characteristic of the eighteen-forties, that things could not remain as they were. Recently there had been widespread feeling, he remarked, that, though advances had been made, the rate of progress was too slow. The *Deutsche Zeitung* was to be directed against the two extremes, against 'the timorousness of a policy of conservatism' which 'paralyses people's courage to sweep away even the real and generally recognised obstacles to the creation of national consciousness and strength' and equally against the 'foolhardiness of revolutionary impatience' which threatened 'to break over existing institutions like a storm let loose.'[3]

The task of the *Deutsche Zeitung* was to speed up Germany's advance to constitutional democracy within the framework of monarchy: 'Therefore we shall campaign for the principle of constitutional monarchy . . . in all its consequences and for all parts of the fatherland.'[4] Only on this basis was it possible to ensure progress towards democracy without running the risk of revolutionary upheaval. Like the academic and scientific conferences, the paper was to contribute to the realisation of this ideal as an organ of public opinion in the 'movement towards public discussion, activity, reform.'[5]

[1] The draft is printed in full in *ibid.*, p. 534 seq.
[2] *Ibid.*, p. 534.   [3] *Ibid.*, p. 535.   [4] *Ibid.*, p. 539.
[5] *Ibid.*, p. 534.

Gervinus presented the issue as standing above narrow class-interests. 'Just as to-day,' he wrote, 'there can no longer be privileged classes in the ecclesiastical state, there can likewise be none in the secular state. . . . The individual is less than ever dependent on his class (*Stand*); it is rather the class that depends on the individual and his qualities. The power and predominance of one class over the other is giving way to more general reasonableness and humanity. The notion of a common citizenship in which the formerly divided classes are absorbed on a basis of equality is the true victor over the medieval hierarchies and the founder of the modern age.'[1] The struggles of the present time, he continued, 'are concerned with achieving full recognition for this new relationship, although naturally the vestiges of feudalism fight against it. What is incomprehensible is that the extreme wing of liberalism itself has recently been protesting against it in those adventurous doctrines which, while campaigning for the principle of class-equality, betray the revolutionary lust to place one single class against and above all others.'[2] This 'new relationship' implied the equal partnership of the bourgeoisie, shielded by the power of the state in the form of constitutional monarchy. What he clearly had in mind might be described in some words from the *Kölnische Zeitung* about the same time: 'It would seem as though a time is about to begin which sees, as the goal of its endeavours, the idea of a state in which law will emerge from the free interplay and interaction of the different interests and circles but will then rule from above . . . with irresistible authority guaranteed by a strong and appropriately organised administration.'[3]

Gervinus believed that constitutional monarchy alone could provide the necessary authority to maintain order in the state, but—and this was a frequent theme of the German liberals—he stressed that it should recognise the need to make concessions. Otherwise the result would be to block 'the natural development of the whole nation.'[4]

[1] *Ibid.*, p. 54.   [2] *Ibid.*, p. 541.

[3] Quoted by Karl Buchheim, *Die Stellung der Kölnischen Zeitung im vormärzlichen deutschen Liberalismus*, Leipzig, 1914, p. 253.

[4] Ippel, p. 535.

That is to say, as the context of this remark clearly indicates, it would provoke the very type of revolutionary activity from below which Gervinus was most anxious to obviate. Reforms from above and opportunity for public discussion— these were among the prime necessities in Gervinus' view for ensuring a healthy development in society. To them must be added a strong and dynamic sense of national consciousness.

He was careful to contrast the nationalism underlying the plan for the *Deutsche Zeitung* with that of earlier decades. 'How much more healthy and more genuine,' he said, 'has this national feeling become than it was in the period of self-conscious teutonism and of Romantic patriotism.'[1] He praised the more dynamic and extrovert nationalism of the eighteen-forties as the reflection of 'the feeling of common purpose and unity in the German nation'[2]; 'how the Customs Union for the first time linked common hopes to common interests!'[3]   To strengthen it was, he explained, one of the tasks of the *Deutsche Zeitung*. He saw clearly the reasons for the change, that it was conditioned by economic developments. It was an important part of his argument that this vigorous nationalism could be the means on the one hand of activising the timorous conservatism of German politics, on the other of curbing the revolutionary zeal of the discontented.

The demand of the German bourgeoisie in this period for a government willing to make concessions to liberalism but at the same time strong enough to keep order at home went hand in hand with the demand that it should be no less energetic in championing German rights in relationship to foreign states. Wilhelm Schulz's book *German Unity through the Representation of the People* (1832) has one chapter significantly entitled 'The Necessity of the Representation of the People in Germany as a Means of Preserving Internal Peace and as a Protection against Foreign Countries.' In 1842 Pfizer, similarly combining the case for constitutional democracy with thoughts of national power, had declared that popular representation was the

---

[1] *Ibid.*, p. 537.   [2] *Ibid.*, p. 536.   [3] *Ibid.*, p. 537.

only means of fostering a strong sense of nationality.[1]
He was writing, he had pointed out, in a time of peace,
adding: 'Germany's present peace is perhaps only the quiet
before the storm, for a new national enemy, in addition to
France which hungers to satisfy her selfish desires at
Germany's expense, is arising in the Slav peoples, and the
party in France, from which many in Germany expect
salvation, would hardly disdain to make common cause
with them against Germany.'[2]   It is true, Pfizer added,
that the Customs Union provides a basis of unity, which
Germany needed for her defence, but 'only a Customs
Union in which the peoples within it have a voice corresponds to their just and necessary demands.'[3]   Pfizer's
words reflected a widespread fear in liberal circles in Germany
and we have earlier noted their impatience with the German
Confederation for its lack of energy in foreign policy.
'We in Germany,' said Gervinus, 'lack an active foreign
policy conducted in the name of the whole, we lack a common
capital where the business of foreign diplomacy could be
concentrated, we lack a central government . . . we lack
a central organ of the press in which this action and reaction
between our own country and foreign states could be
mirrored.'[4]   Such language was also used in some of the
academic conferences, though not always expressed with
this urgency and ardour.   The remarks of Gervinus throw
light on some of the factors in this attitude that might
otherwise be overlooked.

The development of trade and manufacture, the growing
competition in the European markets, fear of France and
Russia, played a major part in stimulating German nationalism in the eighteen-forties.   It is important also not to
overlook the social developments inside Germany,
affecting the relations of the bourgeoisie to the new
class that was rapidly taking shape.   Much that was
truly progressive in German liberalism before 1848 had
its origin in the position of the bourgeoisie as a rising class
seeking emancipation from what was proving an increasingly
restrictive economic and social order—as Marx and Engels

[1] *Gedanken über Recht, Staat und Kirche*, Stuttgart, 1842, II, p. 229.
[2] *Ibid.*, p. 236.   [3] *Ibid.*, pp. 238-9.   [4] Ippel, p. 537.

said in the *Communist Manifesto* in 1848, the European
bourgeoisie had 'created more massive and more colossal
productive forces than have all preceeding generations
together.' But 'the middle classes, like the sorcerer's
apprentice in the fairy story when the spirits he had conjured up got beyond his control, took fright at the momentum
of the economic and intellectual evolution they had set in
motion.'[1] In defending itself in turn against the 'mob,'
it began on the one hand to move in the direction of a
coercive attitude, jeopardising many of its own liberal
principles, on the other to look for means of diverting energy
from the sharpening social struggles at home by focussing
attention on great 'national' issues that might have the
appearance of transcending self or class. There was
emerging a longing to be matched with great hours in which
'we think no more . . . of our mutual hatreds . . . we
are a band of brothers standing side by side.'[2] Thus,
Heinrich von Gagern, looking back over the events of
1848–9, could declare that 'a war with Russia would have
been most popular in Germany; it would have been the
means to settle the seething elements,'[3] and on 6th March,
1849, Haym—convinced of the need to suppress unrest
among the masses—urged war against Denmark and
Russia because 'a bold decision in this direction will pros-
trate Germany at the feet of our king and a severe and
great war will have a purifying and invigorating effect on
the degenerate spirit of our nation which became thoroughly
debased amid the anarchy of the past year.'[4]

This need for national unity, for a focal point of national
feeling, a forum of national values is one of the main themes
of the prospectus for the *Deutsche Zeitung*. This was an
underlying ideal of the academic and scientific conferences,
but Gervinus developed it with explicit reference to the
dangers of the internal situation from the point of view of the

[1] Taylor (ed.), *op. cit.*, p. 24.

[2] Gilbert Murray, 'First Thoughts on the War,' in *Faith, War and
Policy*, 1918, p. 4.

[3] Quoted by Roy Pascal, 'The Frankfort Parliament, 1848, and the
Drang nach Osten,' in the (US) *Journal of Modern History*, June, 1946,
p. 109.

[4] Hans Rosenberg (ed.), *Ausgewählter Briefwechsel Rudolf Hayms*, Berlin
and Leipzig, 1930, p. 75.

bourgeoisie. 'And the essential thing,' he wrote, 'is this: through the absence of a clear position of the nation in its relations with foreign countries and of a corresponding active policy, in which the opinion of the people is heard, an exclusive and disproportionate emphasis is laid in the ventilation of public matters on the internal situation, and our opposition must inevitably assume a more wicked character than is the case with the opposition in all those countries where not only a part of the passion which no vigorous people can lack is shifted outwards, but where also a powerful counterweight is provided against inner divisions by the fact that at every small instigation the nation in its entirety draws together in complete harmony to face the world outside—a counterweight which for us is as good as absent.'[1] The Schleswig-Holstein crisis— which played a part with the 'Germanisten' such as entitles us to regard it as the culminating issue in the academic conferences—was just such an occasion: Gervinus wrote: 'How rarely has such an occasion been granted to us like the recent Schleswig-Holstein affair, in which rulers and ruled, opposition thinkers and conservatives, joined hands and were of one mind! and yet a single such hour is worth more for the inspiration of the nation and can repair more damage than the battles, month after month, of the internal parties . . .'[2]

That one of the foremost German intellectuals spoke in these terms at this particular juncture was no coincidence. Owing to the rapid increase of mechanisation in Europe since 1815 a series of crises of over-production had laid the basis for continued social unrest, while in the 'forties 'conditions in Germany deteriorated for the great mass of the people, partly for reasons effective in all countries going through the phase of early industrial capitalism, and partly because of the relative backwardness of German industry and the coincidence of the emancipation of the peasants with the development of factory capitalism.'[3] 'The complaint of the continued pauperisation,' a writer stated from Western

[1] *Ibid.*, p. 537.   [2] *Ibid.*, p. 538.

[3] Jürgen Kuczynski, *A Short History of Labour Conditions in Germany, 1800 to the Present Day*, London, 1945, pp. 38–9.

Germany in 1848, 'of whole classes of society, while the national wealth is undoubtedly increasing, is heard today everywhere, and it needs only one glance into real life in order to convince one of its justification.'[1] The term 'the hungry 'forties' is applicable to Germany as to other countries in Europe, and in 1846 and 1847 bad harvests there aggravated the situation. In 1848 the June days in Paris were to bring the open clash between bourgeoisie and proletariat which was to serve as a stark warning to the European bourgeoisie as a whole. These facts help to show that the appearance of Gervinus' plan for the *Deutsche Zeitung* in 1847 has more than a chance significance.

It is true that he insisted that constitutional democracy was the indispensable means of strengthening the nation, but he implied that the latter was the end, the former only the means. Thus, urging the necessity of giving the Customs Union a democratic basis, he said: 'If we are serious in our desire to strengthen the nation at home and abroad, we have to set about extending and developing this organisation. It is the starting-point of a German policy based on the will of the people (*Volkspolitik*).'[2] Writing in the first decade of modern industrial capitalism in Germany, he was impressed by the possibilities of development and emphasised that the imagination of Germans was already playing with thoughts of a more glorious future. The Customs Union had achieved more than was expected and with it had gone 'a great general movement for a higher national position and the anticipation of a greater independence of our common fatherland, of a fleet, of world-trade, of a world-role . . .'[3] 'The circumstances themselves,' he stated, 'will teach us to guard against being too active with our imagination in this sphere. But the domination of the material interests, which the Customs Union has advanced in Germany, seems to us to be a power which can only grow in the whole and through the whole, a power in which the first step must lead to steps that cannot be foreseen, a power which will therefore force

[1] Friedrich Schmitthenner, *Über Pauperismus und Proletariat*, Frankfurt a.M., 1848.

[2] Ippel, p. 539.   [3] *Ibid.*, p. 540.

state and people, even against their will, into political developments and embroil them in political complications which we can hardly desire but which we need not particularly fear.'[1]

The plan for the *Deutsche Zeitung* was not only significant for the way its German ideology anticipates some of the main features in the outlook of Wilhelminian Germany, but also because the proposals for the organisation of the paper foreshadow the social structure of its ruling class. Gervinus explained that the paper was to be supervised by an honorary advisory council (*Ehrenrat*) which would meet once a year to discuss policy. Its composition deserves careful attention. Those who had agreed to serve on this editorial board were drawn both from the landowning aristocracy and from the bourgeoisie (including a number of intellectuals who had taken part in the 'Germanisten' conferences). This was the alliance which was to be described in action by Freytag in his novel *Debit and Credit* (1864) defending Germany's hold on the eastern provinces against the 'mob' of Polish insurrectionists and which was to become the social basis of imperial Germany.

Gervinus, however, quickly uncovered his own illusions. It was his tragedy that it was only after providing the first significant formulation in Germany of the pre-stage of imperialism that he drew the theoretical conclusions from his own errors. He left the Frankfurt National Assembly during 1848, at the same time giving up the editorship of the *Deutsche Zeitung*. His self-reckoning is reflected in a letter to Haym of 7th December, 1850, in which he explained why he had broken off relations with the *Deutsche Zeitung* and why too he could not accept Haym's invitation to him to serve as correspondent of the *Konstitutionelle Zeitung*:

> I am convinced that we must set up the flag of the Republic; or rather, to put it better, confess our belief in it and seek support for it in order at the right time to establish it and carry it forward to the east. If there is any political salvation for us, this is the path on which we must seek it. I know full well that it can lead to the abyss as well as to the heights, but I regard this desperate gamble as necessary. It was always a great problem for me whether a nation, which has

[1] *Ibid.*, p. 540.

become spiritually and sensuously so lacking in guts (*eine so geistig und sinnlich verweichlichte Nation*), really possessed the capacity for politics at all; and the most recent experience suggests to me that, *if* the nation is to acquire this ability in the future, this can only happen through the concentration of all its powers, not least its physical powers. It is in vain that you will seek to gather together these forces in the name of monarchy and, unless I am mistaken, it will be even more hopeless to try to do so in the name of constitutionalism; but an appeal to the Republic will—not at the moment but *in due course*—rally three-quarters of the German nation and the fright will make the other quarter willing to accept it or render it harmless. Even a person who still fundamentally believes in constitutional monarchy will be compelled and will be able to go with you; he may regard the Republic as a means, accept it as a transition, while others see it as an aim and a goal. For it is still not proved that an absolutist dynasty has ever been able or ever can make a sincere transition to constitutionalism without having gone through the purgatory of Republic and revolution. For I found this too always a great problem, even when I wrote most confidently in favour of reform and against revolution, whether it is possible for a great nation like Germany under any conditions to achieve political maturity and independence *without* revolution. It would have been inhuman to speak in favour of revolution on the eve of the crisis which posed this question in decisive form. For, even though through theoretical analysis one were no matter how firmly convinced that it was inevitable, one would not be able to convince the masses by means of *any* rational arguments of this inevitability. This must be done through grievous experience, which lays bare the guilt of the princes and of their advisers and which makes the peoples disposed to sit in judgment. As for the others, who overhastily and without justification were convinced of this guilt in advance, their useless bloodthirstyness and fury would only have been heightened by such an accursed sermon. As things are at the moment, they seem to me to show that the question of reform or revolution, monarchy or republic, is settled beyond all doubt.[1]

In 1853 a writer asked the question about Gervinus: 'And what can have driven him at the height of a fanatical restoration, to come forth with a confession which was bound inevitably to draw on himself the hatred of those in power, to come out on the side of democracy at the very

---

[1] *Ibid.*, pp. 121–3.

moment when it seems completely destroyed?'[1] He
answered by saying that Gervinus had hoped that the
monarchy could save itself—as he hoped it might—by
making reforms while there was still time, but that his
experience of 1848–9 had shown him that this was impossible. This was already clear from the letter to Haym,
but in the meantime this writer was able to refer to another
work, the *Introduction to the History of the Nineteenth
Century* (1853), which had recently appeared and in which
Gervinus had developed his ideas more fully. The age,
Gervinus frankly recognised here, was one 'in which the
bourgeoisie strives to combine culture, property and influence within itself and in which, in its efforts to do so, the
lower order (*das untere Volk*) presses hard on its heels.'[2]
If his earlier ideas had been dominated by his belief in the
role of the bourgeoisie as the culmination of historical
evolution, he was now fully aware of the one-sidedness of
his analysis. It was, he said, 'the actual greatness of the
age' that 'in our time . . . the peoples are moving in
masses and in all parts and levels.'[3] His statement that
'there are states without princes but not without people'[4]
no longer implied the identification of 'people' with
'bourgeoisie,' for various factors were operating 'to raise
up the lowest class.'[5] The bourgeoisie lacked the opportunity and capacity 'to maintain itself securely in power
as a political class,'[6] but 'in the popular camp' he found
'the strength of faith and conviction, the power of thought
and of decision, clarity of aim, moral stamina . . . everything which gives a historical movement . . . an irresistible
character.'[7]

Consequently in the second half of the nineteenth century
Gervinus stood rather aside from the many bodies of
bourgeois ideologists in Germany who, rejoicing in the
triumphs of Bismarck, regarded him—though he was not
unmoved by the victories of 1866 and 1871—as among the
sorry figures whom history had overtaken. His idea of

[1] Hermann Baumgarten, *Gervinus und seine politischen Überzeugungen*,
Leipzig, 1853.
[2] *Einleitung in die Geschichte des 19. Jahrhunderts*, Leipzig, 1853, p. 15.
[3] *Ibid.*, p. 166.   [4] *Ibid.*, p. 168.   [5] *Ibid.*, p. 173.
[6] *Ibid.*, p. 171.   [7] *Ibid.*, p. 174.

a law of historical development was dismissed by Ranke
as a 'hopeless view of human affairs' which could only make
the historian feel 'paralysed and degraded in his studies,'[1]
and even at his graveside Karl Hillebrand could not refrain
from describing him as 'a writer without style, a scholar
without method, a thinker without depth, a man without
magic or strength of personality.'[2] Ranke too, in the
essay just quoted, declared that 'Gervinus was overtaken
by events.'[3] He went on to explain that while Gervinus
was setting forth his 'ideas or rather fantasies,' 'quite new
forces than those with which he had reckoned' were gaining
supremacy—'the unity of the nation, in which he too was
passionately interested, was achieved on quite a different
basis . . . it acquired a militaristic and monarchical
character.'[4] His essay ended with praise for the 'great
deed' which, overriding all conflicting interests, had created
unity. Thus, Ranke, whose studied aim was objectivity,[5]
found nothing incongruous in censuring Gervinus for his
political partisanship while himself glorifying the achieve-
ments of Bismarck's power-politics. In 1879—a year
after the opening of Bismarck's long and unsuccessful
campaign against the Socialists—a German scholar could
quote with approval Dahlmann's statement[6] that the *Introduction to the History of the Nineteenth Century* was an epilogue
on the past rather than a prologue to the future (*mehr aus-
als einleitet*).

By this time events in Germany were clearly demonstrating
that the emergent imperialist ideology formulated by
Gervinus in connection with the *Deutsche Zeitung* more
closely corresponded to the prevailing balance of forces in
German society than his ensuing *volte-face*. A year after
the *Deutsche Zeitung* was launched, moreover, the events of
1848 were to reveal the highly contradictory character of

[1] *Historische Zeitschrift*, 1872, p. 139.

[2] *Zeiten, Völker, und Menschen*, II, p. 205 seq., quoted in Mehring, *Die
Lessing-Legende*, 2nd ed., Stuttgart, 1909, p. 29.

[3] *Op. cit.*, p. 143.   [4] *Ibid.*, p. 143.

[5] 'We can only exercise a true influence on the present if we begin by
disregarding it and raise ourselves to free and objective scholarship.'
Ibid., p. 143.

[6] Cf. article on Gervinus in the 9th volume of the *Allgemeine Deutsche
Biographie*.

Germany's much vaunted liberal revolution. It is, indeed, time that we discarded once and for all the convenient illusion—reiterated a little time ago by Bertrand Russell—that it was Bismarck who at a later stage gave German liberalism its 'mortal wound.'[1]

The concern so often expressed by the German intellectuals before and during 1848—and reflected in many speeches in the academic conferences—for strict adherence to legality tended to pass over into frank disregard of it if the circumstances demanded it. A striking example is provided by the attitude in the 'Germanisten' congresses to the crisis in Schleswig-Holstein and a comparison of this with the discussion at the Frankfurt National Assembly of the problem of the subject-minorities. Lappenberg expressed a widely-held view when he declared to the 'Germanisten' that no one had the right anywhere to 'suppress any seed of German nationality.' Less than two years later the subject nationalities in Prussia and Austria were clamouring for national independence. The question was whether the liberals would support this legitimate demand—legitimate, that is to say, in accordance with the principles they themselves enunciated—or whether in an excess of national fervour they would range themselves behind their rulers against these essentially popular movements. The majority followed the latter course. Thus, regarding the policy to be pursued in the matter of the Polish minority in West Prussia, Wilhelm Jordan bluntly asserted amid considerable acclamation that 'our right is the right of the stronger, the right of conquest.' Legal rules, he added, 'nowhere appear more miserable than where they presume to determine the fate of nations. To employ them for fixing the course of nations is to spread out spider-webs as nets for eagles.' He concluded with the words: 'Freedom for all, but the power of the fatherland and its weal above all!'[1]

The bridge between these two attitudes is provided most

---

[1] Cf. Russell's article 'The Unity of Western Culture,' *World Review*, April, 1949.

[2] Quoted by Namier, *1848: The Revolution of the Intellectuals*, p. 88, reprinted from the *Proceedings of the British Academy*, XXX, 1944.

clearly in certain sections in the debates of the 'Germanisten,' in the arguments regarding the desirability of strengthening the hand of governments and the romantic speculation about Germany's cultural mission and the union of all Germans everywhere. Jordan added the point that in order to civilise Germans had to conquer. The internal social advantages of encouraging Germany boldly to confront the world with her power underlay the '*Realpolitik* of the German Liberals, which masqueraded as high idealism.'[1] The situation has been well summed up in these words:

> But the emergence of the minority question, the claims of the Polish, Italian, Czech, and Hungarian movements, brought the German middle class face to face with an almost unsuspected problem and brought into the open the main political issue of the revolution. Was a new democratic Germany to be created, on the principle of popular self-determination, allied with the neighbouring democratic nations and opposed to the autocracies at home and abroad (in Russia)? In other words, was a real social revolution to be carried through? Or were the liberals to throw in their lot with the autocracies against the subject nationalities and to find a compensation for social subjection in national aggrandisement and conquest? The overwhelming majority of the Assembly was composed of constitutional liberals who felt the deepest respect for the monarchs, small and great; almost without exception, all its members condemned and feared the use of force by the popular movement. It only needed the passion of the frontier Germans and the resolute action of the monarchist armies for the middle class to throw in its lot with its rulers. The material advantages accruing from conquest could be seen, but it is characteristic that these advantages—the acquisition of land, of jobs in the administration, and of commercial facilities—should be slurred over. What is most striking is the emotional compensation created at this time—the exalting idea of national destiny, of German cultural superiority, and all the illusions which veiled reality. . . . In this great issue of 1848 the principles of social reform and national aggrandisement were at grips, and the pattern was made for the solution Germany was to accept in 1866–70, in 1918 and in 1933.[2]

The middle class in Germany before 1848, which created the academic and scientific conferences discussed in this book, believed, notwithstanding considerable unclarity

---

[1] *Ibid.*, p. 50. [2] Pascal, *op. cit.*, pp. 121–2.

and obvious contradictions, in some sort of pattern of historical development through which the force of changing social and productive needs adapts old ideals and institutions to new needs. The situation of the German bourgeoisie in 1848–9 made it difficult, if not impossible, for it as a class to continue with equal conviction to regard history as meaningful in this sense. Dahlmann's readiness to welcome the conservatism of Manteuffel[1] as the 'saving action' (*rettende Tat*) was far more characteristic than that of Gervinus to draw the lesson, however confusedly, of the ultimate triumph of proletarian revolution. To take a single example, of those whose liberalism bridges the gap between 1848 and Wilhelminian Germany few are more characteristic than Haym.[2] From his conviction in 1848 that 'at the moment there can be only one political error—lack of energy that does not flinch from driving back the brutality of the masses with all possible violence'[3] he moved on to belief in the need to compose 'the struggle between bourgeoisie and junkerdom'[4] and from there to the position in which, five years before the war of 1870, his 'deep faith in the power of the national idea' led him to 'welcome very strong action in the direction of the power-political interests (*Machtinteressen*) of Prussia.'[5] By this time German liberalism had compromised the best of its earlier aspirations and many intellectuals found it convenient to refer to the uprising in 1848 superciliously and apologetically as 'the crazy year' (*das tolle Jahr*).

[1] The powerful Minister of the Interior in the conservative ministry of Count Brandenburg and Prime Minister of Prussia 1850–8.

[2] Cf. Hans Rosenberg, *Rudolf Haym und die Anfänge des klassischen Liberalismus*, Munich, 1933.

[3] From a letter to Hansemann, 17th June, 1848, in Rosenberg (ed.), *op. cit.*, pp. 45–6.

[4] *Ibid.*, p. 207.   [5] *Ibid.*, p. 245.

APPENDIX I

DATES AND PLACES OF CONFERENCES TILL 1848

(a) Scientists and Doctors

1822	Leipzig.	1835	Bonn.
1823	Halle.	1836	Jena.
1824	Würzburg.	1837	Prague.
1825	Frankfurt a.M.	1838	Freiburg.
1826	Dresden.	1839	Pyrmont.
1827	Munich.	1840	Erlangen.
1828	Berlin.	1841	Brunswick.
1829	Heidelberg.	1842	Mainz.
1830	Hamburg.	1843	Graz.
1831	(No meeting owing to outbreak of cholera.)	1844	Bremen.
		1845	Nuremberg.
1832	Vienna.	1846	Kiel.
1833	Breslau.	1847	Aix-la-Chapelle.
1834	Stuttgart.	1848	(No meeting.)

(b) Classical Philologists, etc.

1838	Nuremberg.	1844	Dresden.
1839	Mannheim.	1845	Darmstadt.
1840	Gotha.	1846	Jena.
1841	Bonn.	1847	Basel.
1842	Ulm.	1848	(No meeting.)
1843	Cassel.		

(c) 'Germanisten'

1846	Frankfurt a.M.	1848	(No meeting.)
1847	Lübeck.		

APPENDIX II

Dr. Otto Abel (Berlin).
Dr. Ahlmann (Kiel).
Hofrat und Prof. Dr. Albrecht (Leipzig).*
Kanzleirat Althof (Detmold).
Senator Dr. Arning (Hamburg).
Dr. Asher (Berlin).
Hans Freiherr von Aufsess aus Aufsess (bei Bamberg).
Thomas Baufield (England).
Dr. Baumeister (Hamburg).
Dr. Bausch (Büdingen).
Dr. Beck (Nuremberg).
Dr. Carl Ferdinand Becker (Offenbach).
Aktuar D. J. H. Behn (Lübeck).
Dr. Th. Behn (Lübeck).
Major Behrens (Lübeck).
Bell (London).
Regierungsrat Bergius (Breslau).
Geheimer Justizrat Prof. Dr. Beseler (Greifswald).*
Landgerichts-Präsident Bessel (Saarbrück).
Dr. Bethmann (Berlin).
John Betts (London).
Advokat H. Biernatzki (Altona).
Advokat Dr. G. Binding.
Geheimer Justizrat u. Prof. Dr. Blume (Bonn).
Stadtdirektor Bode (Brunswick).
Bibliothekar Dr. Böhmer.
Advokat Bopp (Darmstadt).
Dr. Bothe (Ludwigslust).
Advokat Dr. L. Braunfels.
Senator Dr. Brehmer (Lübeck).
Dr. Buchka (Rostock).
Oberappellationsrat Burckhardi (Kiel).
Pastor Burchkardi (Heiligenhausen).
Dr. jur. Burckhardt (Basel).
Prof. Dr. von Calker (Bonn).
Kandidat Carstens (Lübeck).
Prof. Cäsar (Marburg).
Hofgerichts-Direktor Christ (Rastadt).*
Ministerial-Rat Christ (Karlsruhe).
Prof. Dr. Christiansen (Kiel).
Prof. Dr. Joh. Classen (Lübeck).

[1] This is a combined list of those attending either of the conferences or both. Names and titles are printed as they appear in the original list. An asterisk denotes a person who was also a member of the Frankfurt National Assembly.

Cleasby (England).
Prof. Dr. Contzen (Würzburg).
Direktor u. Prof. Dr. Crain (Wismar).
Dr. Theodor Creizenach.
Prof. Dr. Cuntz (Wiesbaden).
Senator Dr. Curtius (Lübeck).
Dr. Georg Curtius (Berlin).
Prorektor Curtze (Corbach).
Hofrat Prof. Dahlmann (Bonn).*
Advokat Dareste (Paris).
Hofrat u. Prof. Dr. Dedekind (Brunswick).
Prof. Dr. Deecke (Lübeck).*
Collaborator Dr. Dettmer (Lübeck).
Dr. Lorenz Diefenbach (Offenbach).
Prof. Dr. Dieffenbach (Friedberg).
Dr. Diehl (Giessen).
Dr. Dietz (Bonn).
Kanzleisekretär Dr. Dittmar (Lübeck).
Dr. Donandt (Bremen).
Prof. Dorner (Königsberg).
Prokurator Dr. C. v. Duhn (Lübeck).
Bibliothekar Dr. Dünzer (Cologne).
Syndikus Dr. Elder (Lübeck).
Etatsrat u. Ober-Gerichtsrat Esmarch (Schleswig).*
Kammerherr Baron C. v. Estorff (Göttingen).
Advokat und Notar Dr. Euler.
Estatsrat u. Prof. Dr. Falck (Kiel).
Archivar u. Advocat Falkmann (Detmold).
Prof. Dr. Fallati (Tübingen).*
Geheimrat Fallenstein (Heidelberg).
Hofrat u. Prof. Dr. Fein (Jena).
Dr. H. Feussner (Hanau).
Prof. Firnhaber (Wiesbaden).
Obergerichts-Anwalt Fischer (Birkenfeld).
Dr. Ernst Förster (Munich).
Oberlehrer Fritsch (Wetzlar).
Advokat Fuhr (Darmstadt).
Collaborator Gallo (Hadamer).
Ober-Gerichtsrat Gasselmann (Rinteln).
Prof. Dr. Gaupp (Breslau).
Pastor Dr. Geffcken (Hamburg).
Dr. Emanuel Geibel (Lübeck).
Prof. Dr. Gerber (Jena).
Hofrat Prof. Gervinus (Heidelberg).*
Amtmann Gramberg (Schwartau).
Rektor W. H. Grauert (Münster).
Prof. Gredy (Mainz).
Dr. Gries (Hamburg).

Prof. Grieshaber (Rastadt).
Hofrat Jacob Grimm (Berlin).*
Prof. Wilhelm Grimm (Berlin).
Advokat Gros (Darmstadt).
Protonotar Dr. Gütschow (Lübeck).
Prof. Guyot (Neufchatel).
Archivar Habel (Schierstein).
Oberappellationsrat Dr. Hach (Lübeck).
Prof. Dr. Hagen (Heidelberg).*
Dr. J. H. Halbertsma (Deventer).
Pfarrer Hannappel (Reiffenberg am Taunus).
Regierungssecretär Hantelmann (Ratzeburg).
Schöff u. Syndikus Dr. Harnier.
Prof. Haupt (Büdingen).
Prof. Dr. Moritz Haupt (Leipzig).
Prof. L. Häusser (Heidelberg).
Geheimer Obertribunalrat Prof. Dr. Heffter (Berlin).
Prof. Dr. Hegel (Rostock).
Dr. E. Heine (Bonn).
Prediger Dr. Heller (Travemünde).
Regierungsrat Hellwig (Eutin).
Dr. Helmsdörfer (Offenbach).
Prof. Henke (Marburg).
Prof. Hennes (Mainz).
Dr. Herbst (Hamburg).
Advokat Eduard Hermsdorf (Leipzig).
Prof. Hessemer.
Oberappellationsgerichtsrat u. Archivar Hettling
   (Wolfenbüttel).
Oberstudienrat Hillebrand (Giessen).
Dr. Julius Hillebrand (Giessen).
Prof. Hiltebrand (Marburg).
Prof. Hjort (Sorö).
Justizrat Höchstädt (Ratzeburg).
Julius Höfken (Augsburg).
Landgerichts-Präsident Hoffmann (Elberfeld).
Advokat Dr. C. Hoffmann (Darmstadt).
Advokat Dr. C. W. Hoffmann.
Lehrer Hofmann (Darmstadt).
Geheimer Obertribunalrat u. Prof. Dr. Homeyer (Berlin).
Landschaftssecretär Hornbostel (Ratzeburg).
Syndikus Dr. von der Hude (Lübeck).
Prof. Dr. Hupfeld (Halle).
Prof. Dr. Ihering (Rostock).
Dr. Ingwersen (Altona).
Direktor u. Prof. F. Jacob (Lübeck).
Prof. Dr. Jahn (Leipzig).
Geheimer Staatsrat Dr. Jaup (Darmstadt).*

Dr. Julius Jolly (Mannheim).
Dr. Joncblöt (Hague).
Pastor K. Jürgens (Stadt-Oltendorf).*
Dr. Julius (Berlin).
Prorektor Dr. Kapp (Preussisch-Münden).
Prof. Kayser.
Prof. Kehrein (Hadamer).
Subconrektor Dr. Ad. Kiene (Stade).
Hofrat Kindt (Eutin).
Notar Dr. Klaubrecht (Mainz).
Pastor Klaucke (Hamburg).
Ministerial-Secretär Klauhold (Cassel).
Pastor Klug (Lübeck).
Bibliothekar Dr. Klüpfel (Tübingen).
Geheimer Staatsrat Knapp (Darmstadt).
Dr. Knispel (Darmstadt).
Dr. Knoch (Uelzen).
Hofgerichts-Rat Knorr (Giessen).
J. G. Kohl (Dresden).
Dr. R. Knöpke (Berlin).
Direktor u. Prof. Dr. Kraft (Hamburg).
Hofrat Prof. Kraut (Göttingen).
Oberstleutnant von Krieg.
Dr. Kriegk.
Dr. Krüger (Lübeck).
Dr. Kruse (Elberfeld).
Stadtdirektor Kübel (Wolfenbüttel).
Assessor Kuhlmann (Schwartau).
Dr. Kuhn (Dresden).
Dr. Rudolph Kulemann (Kurland).
Prof. Dr. Lachmann (Berlin).
Archivarius Dr. Lappenberg (Hamburg).
Landgerichtsrat Larenz (Wetzlar).
Oberappellationsrat Dr. Laspeyres (Lübeck).
Hofgerichts-Advokat Ernst Leisler (Wiesbaden).
Domänenrat Lex (Wiesbaden).
Baron von Liljencron (Copenhagen).
Dr. Lindenberg (Hamburg).
Hofmaler L. Lindenschmidt (Mainz).
W. Lindenschmidt (Mainz).
Archivar Dr. Lisch (Mecklenburg).
Prof. Lochner (Nuremberg).
Dr. Lommel (Würzburg).
Kirchenrat Lorberg (Bückeburg).
Dr. Lotz (Hanau).
Regierungsrat von Löw (Wiesbaden).
Oberappellationsgerichtsrat u. Prof. Luden (Jena).
Justizrat Lüntzell (Hildesheim).*

Collaborator Mantels (Lübeck).
Collaborator Dr. C. Martinius (Stade).
Pastor Masch (Demern).
Prof. Massmann (Berlin).
Prof. Matile (Neuchatel).
Bürgermeister Dr. Meier (Bremen).*
Lehrer Adolf Meier (Lübeck).
Dr. Merkel (Berlin).
Justizrat Meyer (Stade).
Rektor Dr. Meyer (Eutin).
Legationsrat Guido v. Meyer.
Geheimer Justizrat Prof. Dr. Michelsen (Jena).
Geheimerrat Prof. Mittermaier (Heidelberg).*
Dr. Th. Mommsen (Altona).
Pastor Mönckeberg (Hamburg).
Archiv-Direktor Mone (Karlsruhe).
Bibliothekar Mooyer (Preussisch-Münden).
Prof. Morstadt (Heidelberg).
Prof. Dr. Müllenhoff (Kiel).
Kanzleirat Ernst Müller (Weimar).
Dr. Fr. Th. Müller (Hamburg).
Prof. Dr. Hermann Müller (Wurzburg).*
Dr. Münscher (Hanau).
Geheimerrat Dr. Nebel (Giessen).
Dr. K. W. Nitzsch (Kiel).
Oberlehrer Dr. Nölting (Wismar).
Dr. Oppenheim (Heidelberg).
Oberappellations-Gerichts-Präsident Ortloff (Jena).
Oberappellationsrat Dr. Pauli (Lübeck).
Prof. Dr. Paulsen (Kiel).
Geheime Regierungsrat und Oberbibliothekar Dr. Pertz
    (Berlin).
Bibliothekar u. Prof. Dr. Chr. Petersen (Hamburg).
Pastor J. F. Petersen (Lübeck).
Bibliothekar Franz Pfeiffer (Stuttgart).
Hofrat u. Prof. von der Pforten (Leipzig).
Prof. Dr. Planck (Greifswald).
Hofgerichtsassessor Freiherr von Preuschen (Wiesbaden).
Obergerichts-Anwalt Purgold (Darmstadt).
Prof. Rancke (Berlin).
Oberbibliothekar und Etatsrat Dr. Ratjen (Kiel).
Prof. v. Raumer (Erlangen).
Prof. Dr. Ravit (Kiel).
Dr. Anton Ree (Hamburg).
Prof. Dr. Reyscher (Tübingen).
Prof. Dr. Freiherr von Richthofen (Berlin).
Assessor Freiherr von Richthofen (Berlin).
Prof. Dr. Rieck (Ratzeburg).

Hofrat Dr. Ritter (Göttingen).
Senator Roeck (Lübeck).
Prof. Dr. Röpell (Breslau).
Prof. Dr. Rössler (Vienna).*
Archiv-Direktor von Rommel (Cassel).
Conrektor Dr. Rossel (Dillenburg).
Franz Roth.
Prof. Rotwitt (Hadamar).
Präsident Dr. Schaab (Mainz).
Prof. Dr. Schäfer (Giessen).
Dr. Schäfer (Dresden).
Dr. jur. Schäffner.
Advokat Dr. Schazmann (Darmstadt).
Prof. Scheidler (Jena).
Landgerichtsrat Schierenberg (Ehrenbreitstein).
Dr. Kurd von Schlözer (Berlin).
Bibliothekar Schmeller (Munich).
Prof. Reinhold Schmid (Berne).
Justizrat Schmidt (Schwerin).
Prof. A. Schmidt (Berlin).*
Geheimer Regierungsrat Schmitthenner (Giessen).
Prof. Dr. Schneidewein (Göttingen).
Hofgerichtsrat Schnitzler (Greifswald).
Dr. Schroeder (Lübeck).
Dr. Schrötteringk (Hamburg).
Geheimer Regierungsrat u. Prof. Dr. Schubert
    (Königsberg).*
Dr. Schultz (Jena).
Conrektor Schulz (Weilburg).*
Dr. Seitz (Giessen).
Prof. Dr. Sengler (Freiburg).
Collaborator Dr. Siefert (Ratzeburg).
Dr. Simrock (Bonn).
Bürgermeister Schmid (Bremen).
Gymnasial-Lehrer Soldan (Giessen).
Schöff und Senator Dr. Souchay (Frankfurt a.M.).
Graf von Sparre (Stockholm).
Hofrat Specht (Eutin).
Syndikus Specht (Eutin).
Conrektor Spiess (Dillenburg).
Bibliothekar Stälin (Stuttgart).
Prof. Dr. Stein (Kiel).
Geheimer Archivrat Dr. Stenzel (Breslau).*
Obergerichts-Anwalt Sternberg (Marburg).
Pfarrer Adolph Stöber (Mühlhausen).
Prof. August Stöber (Mühlhausen).
Dr. med. Stricker.
Appellationsgerichtsrat Ströbel (Wiesbaden).

Sugenheim.
Etatsrat Amtmann Susemihl (Ratzeburg).
Prof. Dr. v. Sybel (Marburg).
Prof. den Tex (Amsterdam).
Direktor Thiersch (Dortmund).
Prof. Dr. Thöl (Rostock).*
Etatsrat und Prof. Dr. Tönsen (Kiel).
Dr. Tolhausen (London).
Bürgermeister Dr. Torkuhl (Lübeck).
Prof. Dr. Trendelenburg (Berlin).
Direktor Thudichum (Büdingen).
Prof. L. Uhland (Tübingen).*
Prof. Dr. Ullrich (Hamburg).
Dr. Ulmann (Weimar).
Assessor Dr. Unger (Göttingen).
Dr. Versmann (Hamburg).
Direktor Vilmar (Marburg).
Freiherr von Vinke (Olbendorf, Silesia).
Dr. de Vries (Leyden).
Prof. Dr. Wachsmuth (Leipzig).
Kanzler Dr. von Wächter (Stuttgart).
Prof. Philipp Wackernagel (Wiesbaden).
Prof. Wilhelm Wackernagel (Basel).
Dr. phil. Wagner (Darmstadt).
Prof. Dr. Waitz (Kiel).*
Landsyndikus Walter (Ratzeburg).*
Bibliothekar Walter (Darmstadt).
Hofrat Prof. Dr. Warnkönig (Tübingen).
Dr. Weber (Heidelberg).
C. F. Wehrmann (Lübeck).
Dr. Weismann.
Hofrat Dr. Welcker (Heidelberg).*
Staatsrat Baron von Westreenen de Tielhandt (Hague).
Prof. Wetzel (Marburg).
Stadtgerichts-Direktor Dr. Wigand (Wetzlar).
Prof. Dr. Wilda (Breslau).
Secretär Dr. Winckler (Lübeck).
Bürgermeister C. W. Wippermann (Cassel).*
Dr. Wolf (Brussels).
Dr. Wolffson (Hamburg).
Prof. Wurm (Hamburg).*
Oberst v. Wurstenberger (Berne).
Dr. Zais (Wiesbaden).

INDEX

ABEL, Karl von, 74
Acton, Lord, 92
Albert, Prince, 61, 66
Andree, Karl, 9
d'Angely, Regnauld de St. Jean, 22
Antinori, Vincenzio, 44
Arndt, Ernst Moritz, 84, 88, 111
Auerbach, Berthold, 29

BABBAGE, Charles, 45–6
Bacon, Francis, 48
Baumgarten, Hermann, 134
Béranger, Pierre Jean de, 22
Beseler, Georg, 18, 84, 88, 101, 109
Bethmann, Ludwig Konrad, 118
Beyschlag, Willibald, 3, 27
Birch-Pfeiffer, Charlotte, 29
Bismarck, Otto, 134, 135, 136
Bonaparte, Carlo, 44
Börne, Ludwig, 16
Bowring, Sir John, 44
Brewster, Sir David, 45
Büchner, Georg, 8
Buhl, Karl, 9

CARUS, Carl Gustav, 31
Christ, Prof, 102, 113
Christian VII, of Denmark, 110
Coburg-Gotha, Duke of, 61, 66
Cumberland, Duke of, 43

DAHLMANN, Friedrich Christoph, 7,
    17–18, 84, 91, 110, 111, 114, 116,
    118, 123, 124–5, 135, 138
Decandolle, Alphonse, 41
Delbrück, Rudolf von, 89
Derichelet, 41
Diesterweg, Friedrich Adolf
    Wilhelm, 54
Dove, Alfred, 28
Dürer, Albrecht, 13

ECKERMANN, Johann Peter, 38
Eichendorff, Joseph von, 3, 93
Eichhorn, Johann Albrecht
    Friedrich, 82
Engels, Friedrich, 8, 11, 12, 25, 90,
    128
Ernst August, King of Hanover, 51
Ewald, Georg Heinrich August, 52
Eyck, Erich, 10

FEUERBACH, Ludwig, 25, 26, 27
Fichte, Immanuel Hermann, 66
Forster, Georg, 91, 121

Frederick the Great, 22
Frederick William III, 2, 28, 42
Frederick William IV, 10, 27, 61
Freiligrath, Ferdinand, 12
Freytag, Gustav, 34, 132
Fries, Jakob Friedrich, 35

GAGERN, Heinrich von, 129
Gaupp, Friedrich Ludwig, 103–4,
    105
Gauss, Karl Friedrich, 28
Gay-Lussac, Louis Joseph, 28
Gervinus, Georg Gottfried, 12,
    17–8, 29, 84, 85, 86, 88, 91, 92, 94,
    114, 121 seq.
Goethe, Johann Wolfgang, 22, 33,
    38
Grimm, Jakob, 52, 81, 83, 84, 86,
    87, 92, 95, 98–9, 111, 114, 115,
    117, 118
Grimm, Wilhelm, 52, 84, 96–7, 98
Gutzkow, Karl, 9, 16, 19

HAAS, Friedrich, 116
Hansemann, David, 6, 114, 138
Häusser, Ludwig David, 18
Haym, Rudolf, 27, 129, 132, 134,
    138
Hecker, Friedrich, 123
Heeren, Arnold, 95
Hegel, Georg Wilhelm Friedrich, 6,
    9, 26, 54, 101
Hegel, Karl, 92, 110
Heine, Heinrich, 16, 26
Henle, Jakob, 29–30
Hermann, Gottfried, 59, 61, 79
Herwegh, Georg, 12
Hess, Moses, 8
Hillebrand, Karl, 135
Howarth, O. J. R., 46
Humboldt, Alexander von, 22, 28,
    29, 34, 36, 37–8, 41, 42, 43, 52
Humboldt, Wilhelm von, 28

IMMERMANN,, Karl, 7, 9

JACOBS, Friedrich, 70–2, 76
Jahn, Friedrich Ludwig, 13
Johnston, James F. W., 46
Jordan, Wilhelm, 136–7

KAMPTZ, Karl von, 42
Kohlrausch, Friedrich, 51, 61–2
Kügelgen, Wilhelm von, 8
Kussmaul, Adolf, 29

LACHMANN, Karl, 84
Lappenberg, Johann Martin, 36, 84, 111, 115, 136
Laube, Heinrich, 20, 27
Leopold II, of Tuscany, 44
Liebig, Justus von, 28
Luther, Martin, 13

MANTEUFFEL, Otto Theodor, Freiherr von, 138
Marheineke, Philipp, 26
Marx, Karl, 8, 25, 49, 93, 128
Mathy, Karl, 123
Meinecke, Friedrich, 1, 2, 88
Melanchton, Philipp, 70
Mendelssohn, Felix, 61
Metternich, 3
Mevissen, Gustav von, 114
Mittermaier, Karl Joseph Anton, 35, 81, 84, 90, 100–2, 104–5, 106, 111, 123–4
Modena, Duke of, 45
Montgelas, Graf von, 53
Müller, Otfried, 61
Mundt, Theodor, 91
Murray, Gilbert, 129

NAMIER, L. B., 136
Napoleon, 2, 3, 4, 17, 23, 84, 88, 89, 95, 98
Nebenius, Karl Friedrich, 5
Newton, Sir Isaac, 47
Niebuhr, Berthold George, 22

OETTINGEN-WALLERSTEIN, Ludwig von, 75
Oken, Lorenz, 20 seq., 60, 73, 85, 86

PASCAL, Roy, 137
Paul, Jean, 22
Pertz, Georg Heinrich, 84, 86, 93, 111
Pfeuffer, Karl von, 29–30
Pfizer, Paul, 10, 127–8
Pfordten, Freiherr von der, 106
Prutz, Robert, 12

RANKE, Ferdinand, 52
Ranke, Leopold von, 52, 66, 84, 86, 93, 107, 117, 134
Rehberg, August Wilhelm, 9, 101
Reyscher, A. L., 15, 81–2, 84, 85, 97, 100, 111
Riehl, Wilhelm Heinrich, 19
Ritschl, Albrecht, 52, 60, 61

Rosenkranz, Karl, 11
Rost, Dr, 52, 56, 65
Rotteck, Karl, 17–8, 19, 35, 92
Ruge, Arnold, 7, 27
Russell, Bertrand, 136

SAINT-HILAIRE, Geoffrey, 37
Savi, Paoli, 44
Savigny, Friedrich Karl von, 93, 98, 99, 100
Schelling, Friedrich Wilhelm Joseph, 25, 26
Schenk, Eduard von, 14
Schlegel, August Wilhelm, 61
Schmalz, Theodor Anton Heinrich, 22
Schmidt, Adolf, 82, 84, 111
Schnabel, Franz, 20, 92
Schön, Freiherr von, 17
Schulz, Johannes, 74
Schulz, Wilhelm, 5, 127
Siemens, J. G., 6
Simon, Heinrich, 11
Sophocles, 61
Spohr, Ludwig, 61
Spratt, Bishop, 33
Stein, Freiherr vom, 2, 84
Stein, Lorenz, 8
Stenzel, Julius, 117
Strauss, David Friedrich, 26
Stricker, W., 116
Stromeyer, Louis, 37, 38

TAYLOR, A. J. P., 117
Thibaut, Anton Friedrich Justus, 94, 101, 103
Thiersch, Friedrich, 23, 52 seq., 125
Tieck, Ludwig, 34, 113

UHLAND, Ludwig, 13–4, 83, 84, 88, 97, 98

VALENTIN, Veit, 17
Victoria, Queen, 61, 66

WÄCHTER, Karl Georg von, 106
Welcker, Friedrich Gottlieb, 69
Welcker, Karl Theodor, 11, 17–8, 61, 110
Wilda, Wilhelm Eduard, 82, 84
Willey, Basil, 33
Wurm, Prof., 106

ZEDLITZ, Karl Abraham, Freiherr von, 54
Zelter, Karl Friedrich, 33